FINANCIALLY LIT: PERSONAL FINANCE FOR TEENS AND YOUNG ADULTS

THE COMPLETE GUIDE TO YOUTH MONEY MASTERY, DODGE DEBT, TACKLE INFLATION, BUDGET, SAVE, AND INVEST FOR THE LONG HAUL

BRYAN NICHOLSON

© **Copyright 2024 - All rights reserved.**

The content contained within this book may not be reproduced, duplicated or transmitted without direct written permission from the author or the publisher.

Under no circumstances will any blame or legal responsibility be held against the publisher, or author, for any damages, reparation, or monetary loss due to the information contained within this book, either directly or indirectly.

Legal Notice:

This book is copyright protected. It is only for personal use. You cannot amend, distribute, sell, use, quote or paraphrase any part, or the content within this book, without the consent of the author or publisher.

Disclaimer Notice:

Please note the information contained within this document is for educational and entertainment purposes only. All effort has been executed to present accurate, up to date, reliable, complete information. No warranties of any kind are declared or implied. Readers acknowledge that the author is not engaged in the rendering of legal, financial, medical or professional advice. The content within this book has been derived from various sources. Please consult a licensed professional before attempting any techniques outlined in this book.

By reading this document, the reader agrees that under no circumstances is the author responsible for any losses, direct or indirect, that are incurred as a result of the use of the information contained within this document, including, but not limited to, errors, omissions, or inaccuracies.

CONTENTS

Introduction	5
1. BUILDING A STRONG FINANCIAL BASE	9
Financial Literacy Unlocked	9
Change Your Life With These Money Habits	12
Money Mindsets: Your Attitude Toward Money	15
Your Financial Road Map	18
Money Myths to Stop Believing	22
Exercise	24
2. FROM POCKET MONEY TO PAYCHECK	27
Why Work While Still in School?	28
Income Streams	30
Become a Teenpreneur	33
Understand Your First Paycheck	34
Give the Government What Belongs to the Government—The Concept of Taxes	35
Exercise	37
3. FROM CHAOS TO CONTROL—YOUR FIRST BUDGET	39
Why Budgeting Is Hard	39
Budgeting 101: The Basics	40
Needs vs Wants: What's the Difference?	48
Creating Your First Budget	49
Leveraging Technology in Budgeting	52
Exercise	56
4. BANKING SMART	59
Let's Get Banking	59
Getting Your First Debit Card	70
Online and Mobile Banking 101	71
Protect Yourself From Identity Theft	72
ATM Safety Rules	73
Exercise	74

5. SPENDING WITH PURPOSE 77
   Keep Track of Your Expenses 77
   The Fear of Missing Out 84
   Take Control of Your Spending 85
   Impulse Buying 89
   Exercise 92

6. THE SAVINGS ROAD MAP 93
   The Power of Savings 93
   Set Savings Goals 97
   Set Up an Emergency Fund 99
   Save for Your Retirement 103
   Tackle Inflation on Savings 107
   Exercise 109

7. INVESTING MADE SIMPLE 111
   The Magic of Compound Interest 111
   Investment Basics 113
   Invest in the Stock Market 123
   Exercise 126

8. DEBT-FREE JOURNEY 129
   The Importance of Credit 130
   Good vs Bad Debt 134
   Debt and Debt Management 135
   Credit Cards 101 137
   Student Loans 141
   Strategies to Pay Off Debt 143
   Exercise 145

   Conclusion 147
   References 149

INTRODUCTION

Picture this: You're fresh out of high school and starting your first job. You revel in a newfound sense of independence and can't wait to explore everything the future holds. But as the paychecks roll in, so do the bills, and you're suddenly plunged into the complex world of personal finance. What should you do with your money? Should you save it, spend it, or invest it? And what about debt? Is it worth it, or should you avoid it at all costs? The fear of making a wrong financial move or ending up buried in debt is all too real. Does this sound like a situation you can relate to?

Take a breath; you're not alone.

Studies have found that 93% of teens and 97% of parents believe young adults require financial knowledge and skills if they want to achieve their goals. More importantly, inflation and the rising cost of goods have caused 36% of parents and teens to budget more diligently (Tenny, 2022).

Whether you are still a teen looking for a part-time job, have just finished high school and are entering the world of work, or are a young adult who's trying to manage your finances, you most likely resonate with the following:

- You desire the freedom to live life on your own terms and make your own decisions.
- You don't want to rely on others for financial support.
- You crave the ability to explore the world, try new experiences, and create lasting memories—all of which happen to require money.

But, it's not that easy. You may still be living with your parents, and may even be financially dependent on them. You may be underemployed because you struggle to find the right job with which you can gain experience. Maybe you are struggling with student debts, or you just don't know how to manage your finances effectively due to a lack of knowledge.

If you're reading this, you're likely facing similar challenges. That's where I come in. Hi! I'm Bryan, and it's great to meet you! Not so long ago, I was in the same boat, so I understand the challenges you're going through. I know how difficult it can be to navigate the world of personal finance without the right guidance. But I also know that with the right information and mindset, you can achieve financial success.

This book is your key to financial empowerment. It's a comprehensive guide that will help you reduce stress, gain financial confidence, and set you up for better money decisions. It will teach you to avoid costly mistakes and make you more efficient at budgeting. More importantly, it will equip you with the tools and knowledge to achieve your financial goals and live the life you dream of.

Throughout these pages, I will share with you the insights and strategies that have helped me and countless others achieve financial freedom. It will set you up for a secure financial future.

Before we get into the details, I have a challenge for you: Imagine your life five years from now. Think about where you want to be financially and what you want to achieve in that time. How will your financial situation get you to that point? Spend a few minutes reflecting on these questions, then, turn the page, and start your journey to making your dream a reality.

BUILDING A STRONG FINANCIAL BASE

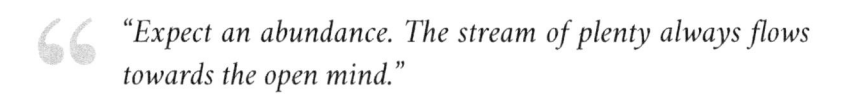

> "*Expect an abundance. The stream of plenty always flows towards the open mind.*"
>
> — BOB PROCTOR

When I was about 14, I desperately wanted the latest iPad. I begged my parents to buy it for me, but their answer was simple: Get a job and buy it yourself. Woah! Where was I going to get that kind of money? I asked my parents that question, and in response, they sat me down and explained the fundamental importance of financial literacy. And that's how I started learning about a healthy financial mindset, money habits, and financial behaviors for success. Let's take things from here.

FINANCIAL LITERACY UNLOCKED

Financial literacy is all about understanding how money works in the world. It's about knowing how to manage your money wisely, make smart financial decisions, and plan for your future.

The Benefits of Financial Literacy

Financial literacy can have a positive impact on your life in many ways. First and foremost, it can prepare you for emergencies. When you have a solid understanding of financial concepts, you're more likely to have savings set aside for unexpected events, such as car repairs.

Secondly, financial literacy can prevent devastating mistakes. Understanding things like interest rates, loans, and investments can help you avoid falling into financial traps that could lead to long-term consequences such as bad debt.

Additionally, being financially literate can evoke confidence. If you feel in control of your finances and understand how to make smart decisions, you'll feel more confident in your ability to handle any financial situation that comes your way.

Moreover, financial literacy can help you reach your goals. Whether you're saving for a car, your education, or tickets to your favorite band's show, knowing how to manage your money effectively can help you achieve your goals faster. You'll know how to prioritize your expenses and make choices that align with your financial goals.

Being financially literate can protect you from bankruptcy and debt. Understanding how to budget, save, and invest wisely makes it easier to avoid getting into financial situations that could lead to overwhelming debt.

Finally, financial literacy can improve your credit score. You can build a good credit history and access better financial opportunities in the future by understanding how credit works and how to use it responsibly.

What Does Financial Literacy Look Like?

For me, financial literacy became important because I wanted to understand my money matters better. This meant understanding different financial concepts, creating a budget, and using financial tools (like apps) to plan for my future. I became aware of different financial risks and continued to learn more about financial principles; I'm still learning about them today. But more importantly, being financially literate allowed me to teach my friends—and now you—about using money wisely.

Pillars of Financial Literacy

Before we go any further, let's get some basic concepts down first.

- **Earning:** Understanding how to make money through various sources such as employment, entrepreneurship, investments, and so on.
- **Saving and investing:** Knowing how to set aside money for future use (saving) and putting money into financial products (investing) to potentially earn a return.
- **Borrowing and managing debt:** Obtaining money from someone or someplace else, using borrowed money responsibly, and managing debt effectively to avoid financial difficulties.
- **Budgeting:** Planning how to spend and save your money based on your income and expenses.
- **Spending:** Making informed decisions about how to use your money on goods and services.
- **Protecting your assets:** Safeguarding your belongings and investments from risks such as theft, loss, or damage.
- **Taxation:** Understanding your responsibility to pay taxes

to the government and how they impact your income and financial decisions.

We'll talk more about each of these pillars in later chapters so that you understand each part of financial literacy properly.

CHANGE YOUR LIFE WITH THESE MONEY HABITS

Money habits are the routines and behaviors that influence how you manage, save, spend, and invest your money. These habits can have a significant impact on your financial well-being and shape your financial future.

Good Money Habits to Develop

I developed several money habits during my teenage years. It would take me way too long to tell you about all of them, but for now, I'm going to set you up with a few.

Set SMART Financial Goals

SMART stands for specific, measurable, achievable, relevant, and time-bound. SMART financial goals help you stay focused and motivated. These kinds of goals give you a clear road map for what you want to achieve and how you plan to get there.

Understand Your Financial Picture

Understanding your financial situation involves knowing your income, expenses, assets, and debts. This awareness allows you to make informed decisions about how to manage your money effectively.

Open a Bank Account

A bank account provides a safe place to store your money and offers access to various financial services, such as online banking, savings, accounts, and loans.

Create a Budget and Track Expenses

Setting up a budget helps you allocate your income toward essential expenses, savings, and investments. Tracking your expenses helps you identify areas where you can cut back and save more.

Build an Emergency Fund

An emergency fund is a savings account that covers unexpected expenses. Having an emergency fund can help you avoid going into debt during tough times.

Save Early for Retirement

Saving toward retirement allows your money to grow over time through compound interest. It can significantly increase your retirement savings compared to starting later in life.

Invest Your Money

Investments allow your money to grow faster than traditional savings accounts. It's about putting your money into stocks, bonds, mutual funds, or other investment vehicles with the expectation of earning an income (called a return).

Pay Down Debt

Timely debt payments reduce the amount of interest you pay over time and improve your financial health. Focus on paying off high-interest debt first to save money in the long run.

Get and Stay Insured

Insurance protects you from financial losses due to unexpected events, like accidents, illnesses, or natural disasters. The right insurance coverage can prevent financial hardships.

Live on Less Than You Earn

Spend less than you earn to save and invest for the future. This will help you avoid living beyond your means and getting into debt.

By adopting these money habits, you can change your life by improving your financial health, reducing stress, and achieving your financial goals.

How to Build Good Money Habits

Building good money habits is important, but that doesn't mean it will happen overnight. You need to work on your good habits continuously. Here are some ways to get started:

- Writing down your financial goals makes them more tangible and increases your commitment to achieving them by keeping you focused and motivated.
- Starting to save early allows you to take advantage of compounding interest, which can significantly increase your savings over time. Consistent saving habits help you build a strong financial foundation.
- Sign up for a budgeting app to help you track your income, expenses, and savings goals. Apps provide a clear overview of your finances and help you make informed decisions about your money.
- Minimize high-interest debt by paying it off as quickly as

possible, reducing the amount of interest you pay over time.
- Checking your bank accounts and credit card statements daily helps you stay aware of your financial transactions. It also allows you to identify any unauthorized or unusual activity.
- Use the 24-hour rule to prevent impulse buying. Before making a big purchase, wait 24 hours to see if it's something you really need or if it aligns with your financial goals.
- Learn about money and personal finance from experts, books, podcasts, or online resources to help you make informed decisions about your money and build good money habits.

MONEY MINDSETS: YOUR ATTITUDE TOWARD MONEY

A money mindset refers to the attitudes, beliefs, and feelings you have about money, influencing your financial decisions and behaviors. Generally, your money mindset will be either positive (abundance) or negative (scarcity).

Understanding Money Mindsets

Money mindsets are shaped by upbringing, cultural influences, personal experiences, and societal messages about money. External factors like economic conditions or financial setbacks also play a role. Luckily, you can change your money mindset with awareness and effort, leading to a more positive and empowering relationship with money.

Types of Money Mindsets

A negative or scarcity mindset is where you believe you won't have enough money or will never know how to use money wisely. A scarcity mindset is characterized by fear, envy, and feelings of limitation regarding money. You may believe there isn't enough money to go around which can create anxiety and envy. In contrast, an abundance money mindset focuses on the positive actions you can take toward your financial goals. Gratitude, optimism, and a willingness to learn about financial management are part of this positive attitude toward money.

Negative Beliefs About Money

Negative beliefs about money usually accompany a scarcity mindset. These beliefs can significantly impact your financial decisions, so you need to change them. Some of the beliefs you may hold include the following:

- Believing that you can't handle money leads to avoidance of financial responsibilities or poor money management habits. This can prevent you from taking control of your finances and achieving financial stability.
- You may believe that wanting to earn money is greedy and selfish, which can create guilt or shame around the idea of earning money. This makes it difficult to pursue financial goals or seek opportunities for financial growth.
- Believing that money is inherently bad can lead to a negative attitude toward wealth and financial success, limiting your ability to see money as a tool for positive change and personal growth.

- If you believe you will never have enough money, you are creating a scarcity mindset which leads to constant financial worry or a fear of never being able to meet your needs or goals.
- Low self-worth or guilt about having money can make you believe you don't deserve to have more money. This prevents you from seeking opportunities for financial growth.
- Believing that saving money requires sacrificing enjoyment or experiences can make it challenging to build a savings habit which may lead to overspending and financial insecurity.

Identifying and challenging these negative beliefs can help you develop a healthier relationship with money.

Shifting Your Money Mindset

Changing your money mindset can have a huge impact on your financial well-being. I know that from experience, so let me share some ways that I made this happen:

- Give money to other people to help develop an abundance mindset that stems from generosity.
- Visualize your ideal retirement to motivate you to save and invest for the future.
- Reading books about personal finance, wealth mindset, and success stories can inspire and motivate you to change your money mindset.
- Believe that success is possible for you to help overcome limiting thoughts.

- Reflect on your past financial experiences to identify and understand your current money mindset and recognize patterns to change.
- Be aware of your thoughts and emotions to replace negative beliefs with positive ones.
- Stop comparing yourself to others. This leads to feelings of inadequacy and greed; instead, focus on setting meaningful goals.
- Identify and release any limiting beliefs about money. Replace them with empowering beliefs supporting your financial goals.
- Practice gratitude to shift your focus from what you lack to what you have.

YOUR FINANCIAL ROAD MAP

As with anything in life, I've learned that planning makes it easier to get to your destination. It makes the journey easier, in short—and that starts with setting financial goals.

Financial Goals

Financial goals are specific objectives you set for your financial future. They can be short-term or long-term and help you work toward financial security. Financial goals are important because they help you prioritize how you spend and save money to achieve your objectives. Setting financial goals helps you understand what financial resources you need in order to achieve them, such as how much to save each month. Having goals also keeps you accountable for your decisions, motivates you to stay on track, and helps with adjusting your strategy if things aren't going according to plan. And when you do achieve them, you can celebrate!

Types of Goals

Short-term goals are financial objectives you want to achieve within the next one to three years. For me, my first short-term goals were saving for an iPad and contributing to my college fund.

Long-term goals will take more than three years to achieve. I planned on buying an apartment and saving for retirement. (And yes, I did get there.)

Examples of Financial Goals

Setting financial goals should be taken seriously, but I didn't always know where to start. It felt like I had so much I wanted to do and save for! Here are some of the goals that I came up with and that may appeal to you:

- saving for retirement using an account like a 401(k) or individual retirement account (IRA)
- learning more about personal finance by reading books and articles, talking to financial experts, and listening to podcasts
- building an emergency fund that covers three to six months of expenses
- opening a store account or getting a credit card to start building a credit profile
- avoiding credit card debt as much as possible, and if it is used, paying it off by the end of the next calendar month
- paying off high-interest debts to avoid the total interest paid over time
- investing money for long-term goals like starting a business or buying a home
- setting career and professional development goals to increase income and financial stability

Setting SMART Financial Goals

For you to achieve your goals, you need to write them out properly, and that starts with creating SMART goals. Remember, SMART stands for specific, measurable, achievable, realistic, and time-bound.

Here's an example:

Save $500 for a downpayment on a car by putting $50 (from a part-time job) into a savings account for the next 10 months.

Specific: Save $500.

Measurable: Save $50 per month.

Achievable: Adjust spending on fast food and entertainment to save $50.

Relevant: A car can be used for transport to a new job or college in the future.

Time-bound: Achieve the goal within 10 months.

Now it's your turn. Write down your first financial goal in a notebook.

Financial Traps to Avoid

It's easy to make a mistake when you are young and not as experienced with money matters. The easiest way to avoid these traps is to improve your financial literacy and learn about potential financial traps. Let's talk about some of these traps.

Skipping Student Loan Payments

A payment missed on your student loan can lead to late fees, increased interest rates, and damage to your credit score. It's important to make payments or explore options for deferment or income-driven repayment plans if you realize you won't be able to pay on time.

Not Creating Financial Goals

Without clear goals, it's easy to overspend or neglect your savings. Setting goals helps you prioritize spending, saving, and investing, resulting in better financial decisions.

Not Saving for Emergencies

If you don't have emergency savings, you can be vulnerable to unexpected expenses or job loss. Aim to save at least three to six months of living expenses in an emergency fund.

Racking Up Credit Card Debt

Using credit cards irresponsibly can lead to high-interest debt that's difficult to repay. Only use a credit card if there is no other choice, and only use what you can afford to pay off in full each month.

Relying on Credit Card Debt

If you rely on credit card debt to cover expenses—specifically, day-to-day expenses—then your income and spending do not match up. Live within your means and use your credit card as a tool to build a credit profile only. Additionally, review your budget to identify the problem.

Getting Into Debt for Luxuries

Taking on debt for nonessential items like luxury cars or new furniture can create long-term financial strain. Prioritize your needs over wants and avoid unnecessary debts.

Not Building a Good Credit Score

A good credit score is important for future financial opportunities like loans or mortgages, but if you don't pay your bills on time, then your credit score will be poor. Keep your debts low, pay your bills, and monitor your credit report carefully.

Financial Ignorance

A lack of financial knowledge may result in poor financial decisions. Take the time to educate yourself about personal finance, as this will help you make informed choices and avoid these common pitfalls.

MONEY MYTHS TO STOP BELIEVING

Besides financial traps, you may also believe some myths about money. These myths won't help you on your financial journey, so it's time to dispel them.

Myth #1: Debit is always better than credit.

Truth: While debit cards prevent overspending, responsible credit card use can build your credit history. Using credit wisely can be advantageous.

Myth #2: Investing is for the rich.

Truth: Investing is for everyone, regardless of income. Starting early and consistently investing small amounts can lead to significant wealth growth over time.

Myth #3: You should buy a home at all costs.

Truth: Homeownership is a huge financial commitment. Renting may be more financially prudent in some situations, especially if buying would stretch your budget.

Myth #4: I'm too young to start thinking of retirement.

Truth: Starting retirement planning early allows for compounding growth. Even small contributions while you are young can add to substantial savings by the time you retire.

Myth #5: Credit cards will always get you out of a financial crisis.

Truth: Relying on credit cards in a crisis can lead to long-term debt. Building an emergency fund is a more sustainable way to handle unexpected expenses.

Myth #6: More income equals more wealth.

Truth: While a higher income can make saving easier, managing finances wisely regardless of your income is important to building wealth.

Myth #7: I have enough in my account to cover my expenses so I don't need to budget.

Truth: Budgeting helps you track spending, identify areas for saving, and plan for future goals. As such, it's never a matter of "having enough."

Myth #8: Financial planning is hard.

Truth: Financial planning can be simple and tailored to individual goals, especially if you use tools and resources to help manage your finances effectively.

Debunking these myths should make it easier for you to make informed financial decisions with the ultimate goal of financial health and security.

EXERCISE

Do the following exercises to ensure you understand the contents of this chapter:

Money Affirmations for a Positive Mindset

Affirmations are statements that you repeat to yourself to help develop a positive mindset. The following money affirmations can help you adopt a better attitude toward your finances:

- I deserve to be financially successful and prosperous.
- Money flows to me effortlessly and abundantly.
- I manage money wisely, and it multiplies in my life.
- I release all fears and doubts about money.
- I am in control of my finances and make smart money decisions.

Choose one or two of these affirmations—or create your own—and write them down on a piece of paper. Place them somewhere you can see them daily and reflect on what these affirmations mean to you.

Quiz

Answer the following multiple-choice questions to test your knowledge of this chapter:

1. What is financial literacy?

    A. An understanding of basic math.
    B. A good credit report.
    C. Knowledge of money management.
    D. All of the above.

2. Which of the following is a SMART goal?

    A. Save $1,000.
    B. Pay off $300 of debt in 12 months by paying $25 per month.
    C. Pay off debts and invest for retirement.
    D. None of the above.

3. Identify the statement representing a positive money mindset.

    A. Money is the key to happiness.
    B. I am in control of my finances.
    C. Money is only for rich people.
    D. I cannot save.

4. What is a good money habit?

    A. Monitoring your income and expenses regularly.
    B. Not having a budget.
    C. Making the minimum credit card payment.
    D. Waiting to save money until you are 40.

5. Which of the following statements is a financial pitfall to avoid?

   A. Getting financial advice from trusted sources.
   B. Creating financial goals.
   C. Saving money in an emergency fund.
   D. Using a credit card for day-to-day expenses.

Answers

   1. C
   2. B
   3. B
   4. A
   5. D

Remember, financial literacy is not about perfection; it's about progress. It's a continuous process of learning how to work well with your money. The fact that you're here, seeking knowledge and self-improvement, is a testament to your commitment to financial success. Now, let's transition to the next chapter where we'll explore the exciting world of making money.

FROM POCKET MONEY TO PAYCHECK

~~~

> *"You can only become truly accomplished at something you love. Don't make money your goal. Instead, pursue the things you love doing, and then do them so well that people can't take their eyes off you."*
>
> — MAYA ANGELOU

When I decided that I wanted to buy some luxury items, I was faced with a new challenge: how to generate an income. I had a ton of options available from babysitting to delivering pizzas, and everything in between. By the end of this chapter, we'll have discussed a bunch of ways to generate income, including entrepreneurship, freelancing, and utilizing your skills and talents.

WHY WORK WHILE STILL IN SCHOOL?

Should you work while in school? It's a good question to ask! You want to generate an income, but you don't want to do it at the expense of your grades.

The Pros of Making Money

Several advantages come from working while being in school. Firstly, it offers a valuable experience that can be beneficial for future career opportunities. A job offers a chance to socialize and develop important interpersonal skills. Having a job alongside school helps you learn to manage your time efficiently, which is an essential skill in adulthood. When you earn money, you improve your budgeting skills and learn to prioritize spending and save for future goals. Overall, if you balance work and school, you earn an extra income and learn important life skills such as money and time management which sets a strong foundation for a successful future.

The Drawbacks of Making Money

While there are benefits to working while in school, there are also drawbacks to consider. One major disadvantage is that working may mean you have less time to spend on studying, potentially affecting your academic performance. Similarly, you won't have as much free time for socialization and extracurricular activities. The responsibility of a job can make you take your schoolwork less seriously. That can decrease your grades, which in turn impacts your ability to go to college, especially if you need to maintain a specific GPA.

Winning Tips to Balance Your Education While Earning Money

You are capable of excelling at school and working; you just need to make a few adjustments to your lifestyle.

Prioritize Commitments

Learn to prioritize your commitments to balance your education and work. Identify your most important tasks and allocate your time accordingly. For me, that meant scheduling study time first and adding work shifts when I had time to spare.

Use a Calendar

A calendar can help you organize your schedule. Use it to plan study sessions, work shifts, and other commitments to ensure you stay on track and know what's happening.

Find Workplace Support

Many workplaces offer support for employees pursuing education. Check if your employer provides flexible hours or study leave to help manage your workload.

Master Time Management

I cannot stress enough how important time management is for everything in your life, and that starts with splitting your time effectively between work and school. Write down your tasks, break them into manageable chunks, and set deadlines to ensure you stay on top of your responsibilities.

Improve Your Organization Skills

Being organized makes life easier because you don't have to think about what is happening when, nor do you waste time figuring out where you put stuff. Keep your study materials, work documents (including your shift schedule), and personal life organized to reduce stress and improve efficiency.

Adopt New Study Strategies

Figure out which study techniques work best for you. It might be creating summaries, using mnemonic devices, or joining study groups to enhance your learning. Whatever works for you, do it to your full ability.

School Comes First

I'll be frank: School is more important than work right now. Getting your education is an investment in your future, so don't let work get in the way. Prioritize your studies, then add a job into the mix.

Align Your Work and Interests

Doing a job is much easier if it is something you are interested in. Your work could be in the same direction as your field of study or it could simply be something that interests you. If your work doesn't feel like a burden, it's much easier to stick with it and stay motivated despite having a busy life.

INCOME STREAMS

Now that you know why you should get a job while you are studying, let's go over some ideas of how you can make money. There are many different ways to earn an income, and I considered several of them myself until I found what was best for me. I'm sure you will find a job that you love too. Here are some ideas for you to consider!

Traditional Ways to Make Money

Let's start with jobs you may be familiar with. You can take up a part-time, after-school, summer, or weekend job, depending on your availability. Consider ideas like tutoring, working shifts at a restaurant, mowing the lawn, or selling handmade items.

Online Side Hustles

If you don't have a transport option—or you just prefer working from home—then an online job is a great option. Sign up for a survey site where you get rewarded for participating in market research studies. Furthermore, you could start a blog or podcast and create content so you can earn money through ads or sponsorships. Similarly, you can monetize your social media accounts by building a large following on platforms like TikTok, YouTube, or Instagram. Freelance platforms like Fiverr and Upwork allow you to offer services such as graphic design, writing, or programming. You can also handle social media profiles for businesses or individuals. If you are looking for something different, open an online store where you sell clothes or other items for a profit.

Offline Side Hustles

Many teens and young people prefer to work in person, and for good reason: so many options exist! You can provide dog-walking or pet-sitting services, babysit children during evenings or weekends, or tutor academic subjects. Also, consider offering car-washing or house-cleaning services for some extra money. Become a delivery person for a company such as Instcart or DoorDash. You could even provide music lessons or work as a youth sports referee or lifeguard.

Business Ideas

Are you someone with an entrepreneurial spirit? Then you may want to start your own business. Yes, you can do it at a young age! Some business ideas that other teens and young adults have told me about include opening an Etsy shop, developing an app, starting a yard maintenance service, and freelancing.

Passive Income Streams

Passive income refers to something that earns you money without you putting in a bunch of time consistently. It's the ideal option if you don't have a lot of time to dedicate to work but still want to make a bit of money. Selling digital products (such as ebooks, Canva templates, or digital artwork) can provide you with money, and you only need to create the item once. Similarly, you can take photos, upload them to image sites, and license them for commercial use. Consider developing and selling an online course on a topic you know a lot about. If you have a website or blog, you can use affiliate marketing to earn a commission every time a sale is made through your referral link. Alternatively, invest in the stock market to earn dividends or capital gains from stock investments.

Tips for Finding Your First Job

Diverse income streams can provide stability and financial growth, especially if you are going through an uncertain time. Let your skills, interests, and available time determine the best way to make money. I also have some extra tips as you search for your first job.

- Talk to people. Networking is important when looking for your first job, so talk to family, friends, teachers, and mentors to see if they know of any job opportunities or can provide valuable advice and insights.
- Choose referees who can speak positively about your skills and work ethic. You can ask a teacher, coach, or previous employer if you've had any informal work experience.
- Use online job boards, company websites, and local classifieds to search for job openings. Then, tailor your resume and cover letter to each job's requirements to increase your chances of success.
- Review your social media profiles to ensure they present you positively. Many employers look at social media when considering candidates, so it's important to have a professional online presence.
- Consider creating a LinkedIn profile to showcase your skills and experience. LinkedIn acts as a professional social media platform for your career, and building it from a young age will give you a strong profile.

BECOME A TEENPRENEUR

If you are anything like me, then you may want to start your own business. It's a challenging endeavor, especially if you are still in school, but it is possible. The question is: *How will you do it?*

Start by identifying your skills and interests. Consider what you're good at and passionate about, as this can form the basis of a successful business idea. Look for problems in your community or among your friends, and think about how you can solve them. An idea that addresses a common issue (and also aligns with your skills) can be very profitable. You can also look abroad for inspiration, explore trends from other countries, and figure out how they can apply to your local market.

Take time to reflect on your ideas by meditating. Meditation can help clear your mind and create a space for creative thinking, which is essential for developing innovative business ideas. It's easy to dismiss ideas that seem unconventional or risky at first, but meditation can help you turn an unrefined idea into a successful business venture.

Have a look at some of the business ideas mentioned earlier in the chapter to inspire you. Other options include creating and selling custom-designed clothing, accessories, or home decor items, providing tech support services to other people, or ordering personalized fitness plans and coaching services.

UNDERSTAND YOUR FIRST PAYCHECK

I still remember the day I got my first paycheck. It was the summer holidays, and I couldn't wait to spend my hard-earned money. So, imagine my shock when I discovered the amount I got was less than what I signed for in my contract. I felt cheated. My manager sat me down and explained why this was the case, and now I can tell you about it.

Your first paycheck might be smaller than you expect because of deductions. When you see your salary written on a job offer, that's your gross pay, or the amount you earn before any deductions are taken out. After deductions, you get your net pay, which is the actual amount you receive.

Deductions can be mandatory or voluntary. Mandatory deductions are required by law, like taxes and Social Security, and are taken out to fund government programs. Voluntary deductions include things like health insurance or retirement contributions, which you choose to pay. So, even if you're offered a certain salary, the amount you take home might be less because of these deductions.

GIVE THE GOVERNMENT WHAT BELONGS TO THE GOVERNMENT—THE CONCEPT OF TAXES

I'm sure you've heard about income tax before. Taxes are fees that individuals and businesses pay to the government to fund public services like schools, roads, and defense. As a working individual, you are liable for various taxes, including the following:

- federal income tax based on how much you earn
- state income tax, which varies by state
- Social Security and Medicare taxes, which fund benefits for retirees and individuals with disabilities

Filing Taxes

It can be daunting to file your taxes for the first time, but it's important to do it correctly. To begin, gather your income documents (like your Form W-2), and choose a filing method—either by paper or online. If you're unsure, consider using tax software or hire a professional tax consultant to help you.

When you file, you'll report your income and deductions to calculate how much tax you owe or if you're owed a refund. Once you've completed your return, submit it to the IRS by the deadline, typically April 15th. File your taxes accurately and on time to avoid penalties and ensure you pay the correct amount.

Legal Ways to Reduce Your Tax Burden or Liability

Nobody wants to pay taxes, but you don't get a choice. It's a responsibility you can't get out of; however, you can reduce the amount you need to pay legally. Let's explore some of these strategies.

Increase Your Retirement Contributions

If you contribute more to a retirement account like a 401(k) or IRA, you reduce your taxable income. For example, if you earn $15,000 a year and contribute $3,000 to your 401(k), you only pay taxes on the remaining $12,000. Plus, you're saving for retirement, which is a win-win!

Contribute to Employer-Sponsored Plans

Another way to use retirement accounts is to contribute to employer-sponsored retirement plans, which reduces your taxable income. Usually, these contributions are deducted directly from your paycheck before taxes are calculated.

Investment Losses

Sometimes, your investments will make a profit, and other times, a loss. When you sell investments at a loss, you can use those losses to offset gains in other investments. It's easier to understand this in terms of numbers. Let's say you made a $1,000 profit on one investment but lost $500 on another. In that case, you only pay taxes on the net gain of $500.

Donate to Charity

When you donate to a qualified charity and itemize your deductions, you can deduct the value of your donation from your taxable income. Unlike retirement contributions, you won't be able to get this income back later on, but you still get the benefit of paying less tax, and you do good for the community. Be sure to keep receipts for your donations to substantiate your deduction.

EXERCISE

Test your knowledge of this chapter with this quiz:

1. Which of these is a benefit of working while in school?

    A. It improves your time management skills.
    B. It helps you focus on your studies.
    C. It distracts you from doing well.
    D. Working is unnecessary; other people can pay for what you want.

2. What's the best thing to do with your first paycheck?

    A. Celebrate by going shopping.
    B. Identify your gross pay, deductions, and net pay.
    C. Give it all to charity.
    D. Spend it on your friends.

3. Why is it important to pay taxes?

    A. You don't need to pay taxes.
    B. To fund extravagant government spending sprees.
    C. To contribute to Social Security and public services.
    D. Taxes aren't important.

4. Which of these strategies are legal ways to reduce your tax liability?

   A. Contribute to a retirement savings account.
   B. Donate to charity.
   C. Use investment losses.
   D. All of the above.

Answers

   1. A
   2. B
   3. C
   4. D

Together, we've explored various opportunities to earn income, whether through part-time jobs, freelancing, or even becoming an entrepreneur. You've also begun to appreciate the significance of understanding your first paycheck and managing your tax obligations. Earning money as a teen or young adult is not just about financial gain; it's about building valuable skills, gaining work experience, and preparing for your financial future. Now, head over to the next chapter, and we'll discuss your first budget, which is a crucial aspect of managing your finances.

FROM CHAOS TO CONTROL—YOUR FIRST BUDGET

> "A budget is telling your money where to go instead of wondering where it went."
>
> — DAVE RAMSEY

I had an idea of how I wanted to use my first paycheck and the ones after that, but it was a bigger challenge than I expected. My spending soon felt out of control, and I didn't keep track of what was going where. I knew what the problem was: I never created a budget. In this chapter, we'll discuss the concept of budgeting, its significance in financial management, and how it is a foundational skill for personal finance.

WHY BUDGETING IS HARD

Ask almost anyone, and they will tell you that budgeting can be tough, especially when you're just starting. As a teen or young adult, you might not have much experience with personal finance, and getting to grips with concepts like income, expenses, and savings goals is a challenge. Additionally, you may feel you need a higher-paying, full-time job to cover your expenses and have enough left over to save. It can make budgeting feel like a distant goal. You may also have a desire to keep up with your friends' spending which creates pressure to spend beyond your means, making it even harder to stick to a budget.

Fortunately, there are solutions and strategies to make budgeting easier and more effective.

BUDGETING 101: THE BASICS

When you choose to budget, you empower yourself with a critical tool for financial success and create a road map to manage your money effectively. Here are some of the benefits you can expect:

- A budget offers a structured approach to your finances and ensures you allocate your income wisely while working toward your financial goals.
- Consistently budgeting and saving can help you build a substantial retirement fund that creates financial security and peace of mind in your later years.
- You can set clear goals and objectives with a budget, prioritize your spending, and adjust your strategy to stay on track.
- A budget helps you prepare for emergencies as you set money aside which decreases the financial stress when unexpected expenses arise.
- Budgeting can help you eliminate bad spending habits because you track your expenses and identify areas where you can cut back.
- Keeping a budget ensures you live within your means and avoid spending money you don't have.

Tips for Stress-Free Budgeting

The idea of setting up a budget is a stressful one, but with the right approach, you can manage your finances effectively and without anxiety. The following tips can help you stay on track.

- **Use budgeting apps.** A budgeting app can simplify the process of tracking your income and expenses which makes it easier to stick to your budget.
- **Don't deprive yourself.** You don't have to give up everything you enjoy when you budget. Allow some flexibility to spend on things that bring you happiness, but keep it within your budget.
- **Give it time.** Budgeting is a learning process, so give yourself time to adjust to your new financial habits and be open to making changes as needed.
- **Track your spending.** Keep track of your spending on a weekly basis to help identify any areas where you may be overspending and make adjustments accordingly.
- **Understand net versus gross income.** You can budget more accurately if you know the difference between your gross income and net income.
- **Account for student loans.** If you have student loans, make sure to include them in your budget and consider creating a plan to pay them off as soon as possible.
- **Manage your rent.** Housing costs can be a significant expense. Ensure your rent is within your budget, and consider finding a roommate or cheaper housing options if necessary.
- **Overestimate transportation costs.** Transportation costs add up quickly so budget for gas, public transportation, and maintenance costs for your vehicle.

Budgeting Tips for First-Timers

The fact that you are doing a budget is great! It's an important step toward a secure future, but it's normal to be apprehensive or uncertain of where to start.

Keep It Simple

When it comes to budgeting, simplicity is key. Although we will look at all these things in more detail later in the chapter, you can get a head start by listing your income sources and fixed expenses, such as rent, utilities, and insurance. Allocate a portion of your income for savings and another portion for discretionary spending. Use broad categories—like groceries, transportation, and entertainment—to keep things straightforward. Avoid over-complex budgeting methods that may be difficult to maintain in the long run.

Base Your Budget on Your Income

Your income should dictate your budget if you want it to be realistic and sustainable. Calculate your total monthly income after taxes and deductions, then prioritize your expenses based on your needs and allocate your income accordingly. If your expenses exceed your income, look for areas where you can cut back or consider finding ways to increase your income.

Avoid Spending Situations

Identify situations or triggers that may lead you to spend unnecessarily and figure out how you can avoid them. For example, if you tend to overspend when shopping online, unsubscribe from promotional emails and avoid browsing online stores when you're bored. Similarly, if hanging out with your friends causes you to spend excessively, suggest other activities like cooking at home to them.

Set Financial Goals

I already told you about financial goals, but it's worth mentioning again. Financial goals help you stay motivated and focused on your budget. Whether your goal is to pay off debt, save for a vacation, or build an emergency fund, having a clear objective can make budgeting feel more purposeful. Break your goal into smaller, achievable milestones, track your progress, and adjust your budget as needed to meet your goals.

How to Stick to Your Budget

It's one thing to create a budget, but it's something different to stick to it. You need to be proactive and come up with ways to keep yourself on track.

Be Realistic

Ensure that your budget reflects your actual income and expenses. Be honest about your spending habits and set realistic limits for each category. If your budget is too strict, you may feel deprived and be more likely to overspend. If your budget is too lenient, you're more likely to miss out on saving because you are more likely to spend the extra money.

Know What You Are Saving For

A clear goal can help you stay motivated and focused on sticking to your budget. Write your goal at the top of your budget and reflect on it frequently to help avoid impulse purchases.

Try a Budget Challenge

Challenge yourself to stick to your budget by trying out a new budgeting technique or challenge every month. For example, you could try a no-spend month where you only spend money on essentials, or you could challenge yourself to cut back on a specific category of spending for a set period. Try not buying candy for a week or make your own lunches instead of buying them. There are many ways to save money; all you need to do is explore them.

Create a Food Budget

While we are on the topic of lunch, you need to realize that food can be a significant expense. It's important to set a budget for groceries and dining out to help you stay on track. Plan your meals in advance, make a shopping list to avoid impulse buys, and treat yourself to takeout once or twice a month. If you know how much you have to spend on food, it's much easier to plan out your meals and treats.

Check Your Social Life

It can be expensive to socialize, so take a look at your social calendar and plan accordingly. Consider hosting a "make your own pizza" night instead of going out to eat, or suggest going for a walk around the neighborhood instead of spending money on the local gym. These strategies require some buy-in from your friends, but if you tell them about your budget goals, you might find that they have similar goals and appreciate the saving initiatives.

Say No

I know it can be tough to tell your friends that you need to save money, but it's something you are going to have to do. It's okay to say no to social invitations or purchases that don't align with your budget. Practice saying no politely but firmly, and remind yourself that sticking to your budget is more important than trying to keep up with others.

Review Your Budget Before Spending

Before making a purchase—especially one you didn't plan for—check your budget to ensure you have enough money allocated for the expense. If not, consider whether the purchase is necessary or if it can wait until you have more funds available. For example, taking money from your budget for an extra night out with your friends isn't necessary, whereas buying medication because you are ill can be deemed a necessary expense.

Budgeting Mistakes to Avoid Making

So far, we've covered quite a few ways to stick to your budget and get the most from it. Now, we also need to talk about some potential budgeting mistakes that you need to avoid at all costs.

Not Saving

If you don't save, you are not setting aside money for future needs or emergencies. This can lead to financial stress when unexpected expenses arise. Without savings, you may have to rely on credit cards or loans, which can lead to debt and financial instability. Additionally, ignoring savings means you're missing out on the opportunity to grow your wealth and achieve long-term financial goals such as buying a home or retiring comfortably.

Being Too Vague

A budget that is too vague may result in overspending and financial disorganization. You need to have specific categories and limits, because if you don't, you may underestimate how much you're spending in certain areas or overlook expenses altogether. In turn, you may experience financial strain which makes it difficult to track your spending or make the necessary adjustments to stay within your budget.

Overspending

Overspending can have serious consequences for your financial health. It can lead to debt, which can take years to pay off and accrue significant interest charges. If you overspend, it may prevent you from achieving your financial goals—or at least greatly delay you. Additionally, overspending may cause stress and anxiety about your financial situation, impacting your overall well-being.

Missing Items

You might forget to include certain expenses in your budget. This may cause you to overspend or you may not have enough money to cover essential costs. For example, if you forget to budget for car maintenance or insurance premiums, you may find yourself unable to afford these expenses when they come up. It's important to review your budget regularly and make adjustments as needed to ensure all expenses are accounted for.

Using Someone Else's Budget

Sometimes, it's easier to use another person's budget plan as your own, but this doesn't mean their budget is suitable for your financial situation. Everyone's financial goals and circumstances are different, making it important to create a budget that aligns with your needs and priorities. Copying someone else's budget may lead to unrealistic expectations or overspending in areas that are not a priority for you.

Budget Procrastination

Many times, we have this idea that we will "start tomorrow," and the same goes for budgeting. You may procrastinate on your budget but that only leads to overspending and financial stress. It's important to start budgeting as soon as possible to take control of your finances and work toward your financial goals. Starting tomorrow means delaying the benefits of budgeting such as increased financial security and reduced stress, which can have long-term consequences for your financial health.

Making Assumptions

A budget based on assumptions rather than actual income and expenses can lead to inaccurate budgeting. For example, you may assume that you'll spend a certain amount on groceries each month without tracking your actual spending, so you don't realize you are overspending. It's crucial to track your income and expenses carefully to create a realistic budget that reflects your actual financial situation.

A Budget That's Too Tight

A budget that's too tight can be unrealistic and difficult to maintain, as it may create feelings of deprivation and increase the likelihood of overspending. It can make it challenging to cover unexpected expenses or emergencies, resulting in financial stress. When you draw up your budget, do so in a way that allows you some flexibility to ensure you can stick to it in the long term.

Not Tracking Expenses

If you don't track your expenses, you are making it difficult for yourself to stick to your budget. Without a clear picture of where your money is going, it's easy to overspend or miss opportunities to save. Track and record your expenses to help you identify your spending patterns. Doing so allows you to make informed decisions about your finances and enables you to adjust your budget.

NEEDS VS WANTS: WHAT'S THE DIFFERENCE?

One of the first things I remember learning as a child is that there is a difference between a need and a want. Needs are essential for survival and maintaining a basic standard of living. These are expenses that are necessary for your health, safety, and well-being. For example, these can include paying for your rent or mortgage, your transport costs, your insurance, your utilities, and even your food. Wants, on the other hand, are things that are nice to have but are not necessary for survival. Many times, a want is an item or experience that adds comfort, enjoyment, or luxury to your life. These can include going on vacation, buying designer clothing, spending money on entertainment, owning a gym membership, or going for a daily coffee and avocado toast.

There can be some overlap between needs and wants, of course. For example, while food is a basic need, dining out at a fancy restaurant might be considered a want. Similarly, while transportation is a need, a luxury car is classified as a want.

To determine if an expense is a want or a need, consider its necessity for your basic well-being and survival. Ask yourself if the expense is essential for maintaining your health, safety, and ability to function in daily life. If the answer is no, it's likely a want. Also, ask yourself if there is a more affordable option instead of the one you are thinking about right now. If there is another cheaper option, go for that one instead.

As you budget, prioritize your needs first to ensure that you can cover essential expenses. Allocate a portion of your income to cover your needs, then use any remaining funds for your wants and other nonessential expenses. It's important to strike a balance between meeting your needs and enjoying your wants to maintain financial stability and well-being.

CREATING YOUR FIRST BUDGET

Now that we've covered a lot about what goes into a budget, it's time to create your first one. I remember when I did my first one: It was exciting and scary all at the same time. Luckily, the process is straightforward.

Step-By-Step

Grab a pen and paper or create a spreadsheet, then follow these steps to create your budget:

1. Start by listing all your sources of income, including wages, allowance, and any money you may earn.
2. List all your expenses, starting with your fixed expenses like rent, utilities, and insurance. Then, list your variable expenses such as groceries, transportation, and entertainment.
3. Subtract your total expenses from your total income to determine if you have a surplus or deficit.
4. Add a savings fund to your budget.
5. Add any debt repayments to your budget.
6. Set your financial goals based on the current state of your budget. Identify any adjustments you can make to reach your goals more easily.
7. Keep track of your spending throughout the month to ensure you're sticking to your budget and to identify any areas where you may need to adjust your spending.
8. At the end of each month, review your budget and make any necessary adjustments for the following month based on your spending patterns and financial goals.

An Example

Here is an example of a basic budget:

Category	Budgeted amount
Income	$2,000
Rent	$800
Utilities	$150
Groceries	$200
Transportation	$100
Entertainment	$50
Savings	$200
Student loan repayment	$200
Miscellaneous expenses	$200
Surplus/ deficit	$100 (Surplus)

Methods to Budget

Budgeting is a straightforward process, but you may be looking for a slightly more advanced strategy that meets your specific needs. Let's talk about some of those methods.

50/30/20 Rule

With the 50/30/20 rule, you allocate 50% of your income to needs, 30% to wants, and 20% to savings and debt repayment. It's suitable for teens and young adults because it provides a simple and flexible framework for budgeting; however, it may not be suitable if you have a high debt or housing costs.

Zero-Based Budget

The zero-based budget is a strategy where every dollar of your income is allocated to a category so that you are left with neither a surplus nor a deficit. This way, every dollar is used purposefully, leaving no room for overspending. Unfortunately, the zero-based budget is time-consuming to manage because you have to track every expense and make frequent adjustments.

Pay-Yourself-First Budget

If saving is your financial goal, then the pay-yourself-first budget is an ideal method. It forces you to prioritize your savings by setting aside a portion of your income for savings before paying for other expenses. You will prioritize your long-term financial goals and create an investment for the future. You need to stay disciplined to stick to the savings plan, however, and must have enough disposable income to make it work. It can be difficult to do that if you have limited income.

The Envelope System

Another option is the envelope system, but it only works if you are paid in cash, otherwise, you will have to withdraw cash to make use of this option. Get an envelope for each expense category and write down the category name on the envelope. Next, place the amount of money you deem suitable in each envelope. Once the envelope is empty, you have to stop spending in that category for the month. It's a great option to track spending on your wants but can become problematic if you run out of money for needs unless you split your needs money into weekly amounts.

LEVERAGING TECHNOLOGY IN BUDGETING

Even though methods such as the envelope system or tracking your finances on a spreadsheet are possibilities, it may be easier for you to use technology, such as budgeting apps. Technology streamlines the process and allows you to automate your plans.

The Benefits of Budgeting Apps

When you choose to use a budgeting app, you are reaping the benefits of technology. Here are a few of these benefits:

- **Real-time information in one place.** Budgeting apps allow you to see all your financial information in one place, including income, expenses, and savings. It gives you a clear picture of your financial health.
- **Automatic alerts.** An app can send you automatic alerts when you exceed your budget or when a bill is due, helping you stay on top of your finances and avoiding late fees or overspending.
- **Easy budgeting.** It's easy to create and adjust your budget on an app. You can set up expense categories, allocate funds, and track your progress with just a few taps on your phone.
- **Track your progress.** Budgeting apps provide visual representations of your spending and saving habits, which allows you to track your progress toward your financial goals. It can motivate you and help you stick it out.
- **Avoid mistakes.** When you use an app, you avoid common budgeting mistakes, such as forgetting to include certain expenses. The app's algorithm can help you make more informed decisions about your finances.

Overall, budgeting apps can make the process of managing your finances easier, more efficient, and more effective. They provide valuable insights into your spending habits, help you stay on track with your financial goals, and improve your financial well-being.

Tips for Using Budgeting Apps

If you search for budgeting apps online, you will be faced with a bunch of different options. You need to decide carefully which one is best for you. Before choosing a budgeting app, identify your specific needs and financial goals. Consider whether you need features like bill tracking, goal setting, or investment tracking. Knowing what you need will help you choose the right app for your needs.

Every budgeting app has its own set of features and benefits. Take the time to compare different apps until you find one that aligns with your financial goals and preferences. Look for apps that offer real-time syncing, customizable categories, and user-friendly interfaces.

If you choose to use a budgeting app—which I recommend—you need to commit to regular check-ins. Set aside time each week (or even daily) to review your budget, track your spending, and adjust your budget as needed. Regular check-ins will help you stay on track with your financial goals and make informed decisions about your finances.

Examples of Budgeting Apps

Budgeting apps are available for all operating systems, and more keep popping up monthly, so it can be tough to choose the right one to use. Even if you're tempted to try a few different apps, select one at a time and stick with it for a month or two before trying out a different app. To make it easier, I'm going to tell you about a few of the apps that I've tried.

Mint

Mint is for just about every financial goal. It offers a comprehensive overview of your finances, including budgeting, bill tracking, and investment monitoring. Some users find the interface a bit overwhelming, though, and mention that transactions aren't always categorized correctly.

YNAB

YNAB, an acronym for You Need a Budget, is a hands-on, zero-based budgeting app. It focuses on giving every dollar a job, encourages proactive budgeting decisions, and offers educational resources. A downside of YNAB is that you need to capture transactions manually, which can be a learning curve for new users.

Goodbudget

With Goodbudget, you make use of the envelope system but in an online way. It helps you allocate funds to virtual envelopes for different spending categories, which makes it easier to spend mindfully. Goodbudget also requires manual tracking of expenses, however, and it has a limited number of features compared to other apps.

EveryDollar

Another zero-based budgeting app is EveryDollar. It offers a straightforward approach to zero-based budgeting and syncs with your bank account for easy tracking. There is a free version, but it doesn't include premium features that you may need in order to budget properly.

Empower Personal Wealth

If you want to track your wealth and spending, then Empower Personal Wealth may be the option for you. The app provides a holistic view of your financial health, tracks your net wealth, and analyzes spending. It does not have as many features as other apps, but it does give you an easy snapshot of your overall financial health.

PocketGuard

PocketGuard is a simplified budgeting app that gives you a clear indication of your finances, including bills, income, and expenses. It also offers ideas to help you save money. Some users find the budgeting recommendations repetitive or not tailored to their needs, however.

Honeydue

Honeydue is slightly different from other apps since it was created to help couples track and manage their finances together. It allows you and your partner to track bills, budget, and sync accounts. The interface can be cluttered or confusing and may not offer as much customization as other apps. Additionally, you need to decide if budgeting with a partner is really the way to go in your current circumstances.

Fudget

Fudget is a simple budgeting app where you don't need to sync accounts. The no-frills approach to budgeting makes it easy to track expenses manually. Fudget doesn't have as many advanced features as other apps, and manual data entry may take longer, but it's still a decent app to use.

EXERCISE

In this chapter, you've learned a lot about budgeting. Now, you can put it into practice by doing the following exercises.

Worksheet 1: Monthly Income and Expense Tracker

Use this worksheet to track your monthly income and expenses. Fill in your sources of income and list your fixed and variable expenses to see where your money is going.

Income

Income	Amount ($)
Job	
Allowance	
Other	
Total income	

Expenses

Expenses	Amount ($)
Rent/mortgage	
Utilities	
Groceries	
Transportation	
Entertainments	
Savings	

Debt repayments	
Other	
Total expenses	

Surplus/deficit: Total income - Total expenses = _____

Worksheet 2: Savings Goal Tracker

Set and track your savings goals with this worksheet. Write down your savings goals and track your progress each month to stay motivated.

Savings goals	Goal amount ($)	Saved amount ($)	Progress (%)
Emergency fund			
Goal 1:			
Goal 2:			
Goal 3:			
Total			

Worksheet 3: Weekly Spending Tracker

Write down your expenses for each category and total them at the end of the week to see where you can cut back.

Category	Budgeted amount ($)	Actual amount ($)
Groceries		
Dining out		
Transportation		
Entertainment		
Shopping		
Other		
Total		

Now that your budget is set, you're not just keeping tabs on your money; you're guiding it toward your financial aspirations. Whether you're saving for an exciting getaway, chipping away at debt, or laying the groundwork for future investments, you're on your way to financial stability and independence. In the next chapter, we'll explore banking. Understanding how to manage your money through bank accounts, online banking, and financial institutions is a vital aspect of financial literacy.

BANKING SMART

> "When money realizes that it is in good hands, it wants to stay and multiply in those hands."
>
> — IDOWU KOYENIKAN

Have you thought about how you will deal with your money? It may seem like an odd question, because these days, everyone has a bank account. Do you have one? I opened my first bank account when I was about 14. I remember feeling like a grown up but I struggled to choose a bank. I want to make it easier for you, so let's talk about banking in this chapter.

LET'S GET BANKING

Whether you already have a bank account or this is the first time you will open one, it doesn't matter. The same basic guidelines still apply. You want to get an account that works for you, instead of the other way around (such as paying ridiculous bank fees).

Choosing a Bank

When you choose your first bank account, you have a few options to consider. You can choose between an online bank, a traditional bank, or a credit union. Some banks can be classified as a combination of these options. Essentially, you need to look for the bank that best suits your needs, lifestyle, and goals.

Online Bank

An online bank offers convenience through its digital platform and allows you to manage your account anytime, anywhere. You will open your account online, submit all your documents, and access your online account to manage transactions and personal details. Usually, online banks have lower fees and higher interest rates compared to traditional banks, which can be beneficial as you start your banking journey. However, since online banks have limited or no physical locations, you may struggle to talk to someone face-to-face.

Traditional Bank

Traditional banks have physical branches where you can open your account, conduct transactions, and get assistance from professional bankers. They offer a wide range of services, including checking and savings accounts, loans, and investment options. A professional banker can also recommend the best account for your needs. A traditional bank typically has higher fees compared to online banks, but that's because they need to pay for the building and staff. Many people feel it's still worth it as you have access to more services and benefits.

Credit Union

Credit unions are member-owned, meaning you become a member by opening an account. They often have a community focus and offer personalized service and involvement in local initiatives. You may have voting rights in the union's decisions, but that depends on what kind of account you have and what the credit union offers. Usually, credit unions have lower fees and competitive interest rates when compared to traditional banks.

What to Consider When Choosing a Bank

Do you have an idea of what kind of bank you will go for yet? I opted to go the traditional bank route because I wanted to talk through the account options with someone. But maybe you already know which bank you want to go with, and all that's left to do is choose the best account for your goals. Here are some things to consider:

- Identify the right account by considering your banking needs and goals. If you need easy access to your money, a checking account might be best. If you're saving for the future, a savings or investment account could be more suitable.
- Look for banks that offer accounts with low fees or waive fees under certain conditions. For example, some banks have special accounts for teenagers under a certain age or for individuals who are busy with their tertiary education. Other banks lower their fees if you maintain a minimum balance or set up a direct deposit.
- A local bank branch can be convenient for tasks like depositing checks or cash or if you need answers to questions quickly. Find out where your closest branch is before opening an account.

- Choose a bank account that offers services and features that fit your lifestyle. For example, if you travel frequently, look for a bank with a large ATM network or reimbursements for out-of-network fees.
- Evaluate the bank's online and mobile banking options, specifically for your account. Loof for features like easy account transfers, bill payments, and budgeting tools that can help you manage your finances more efficiently.
- Read the terms and conditions of the account carefully. Pay attention to fees—both monthly and for individual transactions—and identify any minimum balance requirements. From there, determine if any restrictions or limitations may apply.
- Research the bank's reputation by reading reviews from other customers. You can check for reviews specific to the account you are interested in, or talk to your friends about the accounts that work best for them. Also look for feedback on customer service, account fees, and overall satisfaction with the bank's services.
- Determine which features are most important to you. This could include 24/7 customer support, access to a large ATM network, or incentives like cashback rewards or high-interest rates on savings accounts.

By considering these factors, you can choose a bank that not only meets your financial needs but also provides a positive banking experience that sets you up for the future.

Choosing a Bank Account

Having a bank account comes with several benefits that can improve your financial management and provide peace of mind. Let's go over those first.

- A bank account allows you to withdraw cash from ATMS, make purchases using a debit card, and set up automatic bill payments which makes transactions more convenient and secure than carrying cash.
- Banks offer protection for your money through FDIC insurance or similar schemes, ensuring that your funds are safe even if the bank fails.
- With online and mobile banking, you can manage your account, transfer money, and pay bills conveniently, without the need to visit a physical branch.
- Bank accounts typically have lower fees when compared to alternative financial services like check-cashing stores or prepaid debit cards.
- A bank account establishes a relationship with your bank which makes it easier to access credit products at a later time.
- Bank accounts offer a secure place to store your money and allow you to save easily for short-term goals and emergencies.

Common Bank Accounts

When you open your first account, you will need to choose the type of account that suits your needs best. All accounts have their pros and cons, and you may find that you need more than one type of account as your banking needs change over time.

A checking account is designed for everyday transactions. They allow you to deposit money, write checks (although this is being phased out), use a debit card, and access your funds through ATMs, online, and mobile banking. A checking account offers easy access to your money and allows you to pay bills and make purchases conveniently. Later in life, your bank may also offer you an overdraft facility on your checking account. However, checking accounts can be costly because they often have several fees, including monthly maintenance fees, out-of-network ATM fees, and card swiping fees. Additionally, they typically don't earn much interest, if any, on your balance.

Savings accounts are meant for storing money you don't need for daily expenses. They are a safe place to save and earn interest on your balance. Depending on the specific account, you should have easy access to your funds (although limited withdrawals are allowed each month), the ability to earn slightly higher interest, and know that they are often FDIC insured. Basic savings accounts usually have minimum balance requirements and lower interest rates compared to other types of savings accounts like money market accounts or certificates of deposits.

A money market account is a type of savings account that typically provides higher interest rates. They often require a higher minimum balance to open and maintain the account. Money market accounts do have some restrictions in terms of how you can access your money and the number of times you can do so monthly. Additionally, these accounts tend to have high fees.

Another type of savings account is certificates of deposit (CD), which are time deposits that require you to add money to the account for a set amount of time, ranging from a few months to several years. In return, you earn a higher interest rate than a regular savings account. Your principal amount (the amount you add monthly) is covered by FDIC insurance to ensure you get at least that amount if you wait to cash out until maturity, which is the end of the agreed depositing period. However, CDs tend to have penalties for early withdrawal, so you can't access your money without paying fees until the CD matures.

Each type of account serves a different purpose and offers unique benefits and drawbacks. The right account for you depends on our financial goals, how you plan to use the account, and your tolerance for fees and restrictions.

The Details on Checking Accounts

In all likelihood, you will open a checking account. Even if you opt for a savings account as a teenager, the benefits of a checking account will become necessary later on in your life. Before choosing a checking account, several factors should be considered to ensure it aligns with your financial needs and lifestyle.

As a starting point, decide whether you need a basic checking account for everyday transactions or a high-yield checking account that offers interest on your balance. Also, decide if you want the convenience of online banking or the personalization that comes with in-person services offered by traditional banks with physical locations. The features of the bank's mobile app can also convince you whether it's the right choice for you or not.

Check if the account has a monthly fee and whether it can be waived by meeting certain requirements, such as maintaining a minimum balance or setting up a direct deposit. You should also ask about other fees, including overdraft fees, out-of-network ATM fees, and foreign transaction (international) fees.

Opening Your First Account

Have you chosen an account yet? Before you open it, ask yourself the following questions to ensure you've thought about everything:

1. What types of accounts does the bank offer, and what are their features?

2. What fees are associated with the account, and how can they be waived?
3. Does the account earn interest, and if so, what is the interest rate?
4. What online and mobile banking features are available?
5. Where are the bank's ATMs?
6. What overdraft protection options are available?
7. Is the money insured?

Additionally, keep in mind that the minimum age to open a bank account varies by bank and by state, but most banks require you to be at least 18 years old. Some banks may allow you to open an account earlier, but your parent or guardian will be the co-owner of the account.

Before you go to the bank, get your documentation and details ready. The bank will ask you for the following:

- a valid, government-issued photo ID
- basic information, such as your birthdate, Social Security number, taxpayer identification number, and phone number
- an initial deposit (not required by all banks)
- a co-owner if you're not yet 18
- identification details for other applicants if you're opening a joint account
- miscellaneous information, including the source of your income or employment status

As you get ready to open your first account, remember that you need to research different banks and account options to find one that meets your needs. Compare fees, interest rates, and features, and ask questions if you don't understand something. Gather all your documents before you visit the bank or open an account online, and review all bank documents before signing everything.

Now, follow these steps to open your bank account:

1. Visit your chosen bank or their online platform and complete an application form for your chosen account.
2. Provide identification and submit any documentation required by the bank.
3. Once the application is approved, make an initial deposit.
4. Review the bank's welcome kit or account materials to get your account number, card number, and other information about managing your account.
5. Set up online and mobile banking using the instructions supplied by your bank.
6. Start using your account!

Overall, opening a bank account is a simple process that can be completed in a few steps. Choose the right bank and account for your needs, and you can start managing your money effectively and securely.

Manage Your Bank Account

Manage your bank account effectively by understanding how to use your bank card and its features.

Use Your Bank Card

All bank cards work in the same way: you simply swipe it at a pay point and the money will be deducted from your account. First, debit cards are linked to your checking account and allow you to make purchases and withdraw cash from ATMs. Second, credit cards allow you to borrow money from the issuer up to a certain limit, but you must repay the borrowed amount, often with interest, by the due date. Lastly, prepaid cards are loaded with funds in advance and can be used until the balance runs out.

Make Payments to Your Account

To add funds to your account, you can visit a bank branch and deposit checks or cash with a teller. Some banks have in-branch deposit machines or ATMs where you can easily deposit cash. Use your bank's website or mobile app to transfer funds from another account into your bank account.

Pay Others

You will need to pay other people, as well as bills and places. Use electronic fund transfers (EFTs) to make payments online or through mobile apps. It's not used as much anymore, but you can also write a check or obtain a banker's draft to make payments. If you need to make payments regularly, consider an automatic payment like a debit order.

Overdraft Considerations

An overdraft allows you to spend more money than you have in your account, but it can result in fees and interest charges. You need to apply for an overdraft on your account. The bank will consider your financial situation and ability to repay the borrowed amount before approving an overdraft.

Extra Tips

You already know a lot about using your bank account, but I have a few more tips to offer you below:

- Download your bank's mobile banking app to monitor your account, transfer funds, and pay bills on the go.

- Check your account balance frequently to keep track of your spending.
- Set up automatic deposits for savings and bill payments to ensure they are paid on time.
- Familiarize yourself with your bank's fee structure and avoid unnecessary fees.
- Some accounts offer perks such as cashback rewards; use these perks to your advantage.

How to Check Your Bank Balance

Here's how you can check your bank balance using different methods:

Bank Website

- Log in to your online banking account.
- Navigate to the account summary section to view your balance.

Mobile Banking App

- Open your bank's mobile banking app.
- Log in to your account.
- Navigate to the account section to see the balance.

At the ATM

- Insert your card into the ATM and enter your PIN.
- Select the option to check your balance.
- Your balance will be displayed on the screen with an option to print it on a receipt.

Bank Statements

- Check your monthly bank statement.
- Find the closing balance box.

Via Phone

- Call your bank's customer service number and follow the prompts.
- Provide your account number and other identifying information for security purposes.
- You will be told your balance.

GETTING YOUR FIRST DEBIT CARD

Debit cards are linked to your checking account (which we discussed earlier) and allow you to make purchases, withdraw cash, and pay bills electronically. When you use your debit card, the money is deducted directly from your account, so it's important to keep track of your transactions.

To get your first debit card, you need to open a checking account. Most banks issue debit cards automatically when you open a new account, but you may need to request one. Your card will be available for pick-up at the branch or delivered to you in the mail.

How to Handle Your Debit Card

Treat your debit card like cash and keep it in a safe place. Memorize your pin and never share it with anyone. If your card is lost or stolen, report it to your bank immediately to prevent unauthorized transactions.

Talk to your bank about debit card fees, such as ATM fees when you withdraw cash, especially if you are using an out-of-network ATM. Try to use ATMs within your bank's network to avoid fees, and keep track of your balance to avoid overdrawing your account. Also, ask about fees associated with swiping your card and whether any places offer rewards for using your debit card.

Tips to Use Your Debit Card Wisely

Here are a few more tips for you that helped me with using a debit card:

- Monitor your account and balance regularly to identify any suspicious transactions.
- Set up alerts (on the banking app) for low balances, large transactions, or suspicious activity.
- When using your card in person, use the chip reader if you want to be as safe as possible.
- Be wary of card skimmers at ATMs or card readers. Do not use that pay point if it seems like the machine has been tampered with in any way.

ONLINE AND MOBILE BANKING 101

I have already given you a bit of detail about online and mobile banking, but it's become an important part of my life. Almost all my transactions are done using one of these methods because they're convenient and I have full control of what's happening with my account. Let's talk about them a bit more.

Online Banking

Online banking allows you to manage your bank account over the internet which makes it convenient and accessible. You can check your balance and transaction history, transfer money between accounts, pay bills electronically, and set up alerts for account activity. You can also use your online account to apply for loans or credit cards, access tax documents, and communicate with your bank through secure messaging.

Mobile Banking

Mobile banking lets you access your bank account and perform transactions from your smartphone or tablet. You will get similar services to those offered by online banking. Many banks offer mobile banking apps specifically designed for teens and young adults or offer additional features such as budgeting assistance. If you have a joint account with your parent or guardian, they will be able to add parental controls.

PROTECT YOURSELF FROM IDENTITY THEFT

Identity theft occurs when someone steals your personal information, such as your bank account details or Social Security number, to commit fraud or other crimes in your name. Financial identity theft refers to unauthorized transactions on your bank account or credit card. Identity theft can occur through data breaches, phishing scams, stolen wallets or mail, or malware on your computer or mobile device. The warning signs of identity theft include unexplained withdrawals from your bank account, unauthorized charges on your credit card, or receiving bills or statements for accounts you didn't open.

To prevent identity theft, remember the following:

- Monitor your accounts regularly for suspicious activity.
- Use strong, unique passwords for online accounts.
- Shred sensitive documents before disposing of them.
- Be cautious of phishing scams, unsolicited emails, or calls asking for personal information.

If you suspect you're a victim of identity theft, report it to your bank, card issuer, and the Federal Trade Commission (FTC) immediately. Freeze your accounts to prevent further fraud and monitor your credit report regularly for any unusual activity.

ATM SAFETY RULES

ATMs provide convenient access to your bank account for various transactions, but it's essential to follow safety rules and precautions to protect yourself from theft and fraud. I have a few tips to help you here:

- Use ATMs located in well-lit, public areas, such as inside a bank branch or a busy area.
- Inspect the card reader and keypad for any signs of tampering before using an ATM.
- Shield the keypad with your hand when you enter your PIN. Memorize your PIN instead of writing it down somewhere.
- Stay vigilant and watch out for anyone who appears to be loitering or behaving suspiciously.
- Limit your time at the ATM by having your card ready and knowing what you want to do.
- After the transaction, take your card, cash, and receipt and put them away securely before leaving the ATM.

- If your card is lost or stolen, report it to your bank immediately to prevent unauthorized use.

EXERCISE

For this exercise, I want you to do a hands-on bank account review as well as practice ATM safety.

Activity 1: Bank Account Review

Download an online bank statement from your account or ask your parents if you can review one of their statements. Look through the statement to identify deposits, withdrawals, payments, and any fees or charges. Consider your spending habits and how you might manage your money differently.

Activity 2: ATM Safety Practice

Go to a safe ATM nearby. Inspect it for any unusual devices or attachments, then insert your card if it is safe to do so. Enter your PIN and check your balance. Stay aware of your surroundings. How did you feel about using the ATM? What steps did you take to ensure your safety?

With the right bank account, you've set the stage for effective money management and financial growth. Banking is about where you store your money, but it's also about how you use your accounts to streamline your transactions and protect your hard-earned cash. In the next chapter, we will shift our focus to spending money mindfully and making wise decisions.

MAKE A DIFFERENCE WITH YOUR REVIEW

Unlock the Power of Generosity

"Life's most persistent and urgent question is, 'What are you doing for others?"

— MARTIN LUTHER KING JR

Just like starting a business or learning something new, helping others can make a big difference! And you can start making a difference right now, even if you're still learning about money and savings.

Would you help someone you've never met, even if you never got to meet them? This person is a lot like you, maybe they're a bit unsure about money and looking for some good advice. You've got the chance to help them out!

Our big goal with the book *Financially Lit: Personal Finance for Teens and Young Adults* is to help everyone, especially young folks like you, learn to manage money better. Everything I do is for that reason. And to reach that goal, we need to get this book into as many hands as possible.

Here's where you come in! Lots of people pick books based on what others say about them. So, I'm asking you to help out another young person like yourself by writing a review of this book.

Your review doesn't cost a penny and only takes a little bit of your time, but it can change another person's life in a big way! Your review could help:

- ...one more young person learn to save their allowance.
- ...one more family start planning their spending.
- ...one more student start their own small business.
- ...one more friend make smart money choices.
- ...one more dream of financial freedom come true.

To start helping and get that awesome feeling, just write a review—it's super easy and quick!

Just scan the QR code to write your review:

If you're excited to help out and make a difference, then you're just the kind of friend I'm looking for! Welcome to the club—you're awesome!

I can't wait to share even more cool tips and ideas with you in the next chapters of our book. You're going to learn so much about making money work for you!

Thanks a ton! Now, let's get back to our money-saving tips and tricks.

- Your biggest fan, Bryan Nicholson

PS - Did you know? When you help someone else, it not only makes them happier, but it makes you feel great too!

If you think this book could help another young person like you, why not share it with them? It's a great way to spread the knowledge and help others.

SPENDING WITH PURPOSE

> "Once you really accept that spending money doesn't equal happiness, you have half the battle won."
>
> — ERNEST CALLENBACH

The first time I received money from my part-time job, I was thrilled! I immediately wanted to buy something, but I knew I had to save for some big purchases. *What should I do?* I wasn't really sure. I don't want the same uncertainty to bother you, so in this chapter, we are going to talk about responsible spending and how to align your spending with your goals.

KEEP TRACK OF YOUR EXPENSES

To achieve personal financial success, you need to track your expenses. Diligently monitor your spending to enhance your financial awareness and gain an understanding of where your money is going. This practice empowers you to pay off student debt efficiently, as you can allocate funds strategically and prioritize debt repayments. If you aren't worried about debt, you can save more by decreasing your expenses. As you monitor your savings, you become more motivated and experience a sense of achievement. Expense tracking also allows you to detect potential problems early on, such as overspending or insufficient savings, which makes it easier to correct your actions promptly.

Tracking expenses helps you identify your spending patterns and enables you to differentiate between wants and needs. With this awareness, you can make informed decisions about your purchases and ensure you prioritize your financial resources in the best way possible. Moreover, it makes it easier to stick to your budget, as expense tracking provides real-time feedback on your spending habits.

When you track expenses, it's easier to set and achieve financial goals because you can assess your financial situation accurately and establish realistic objectives. It makes it easier to monitor your net worth. You can also detect and prevent fraud quickly because you are looking at your transaction details frequently.

Unwise Spending Habits

Now that you know why it's beneficial to track expenses, we need to talk about unwise spending habits. These are the kinds of things you need to avoid if you want to use your funds optimally.

Living Beyond Your Means

When you live beyond your means, you spend more money than you earn, often relying on credit cards or loans to maintain your lifestyle. This might not be an issue as a teenager, but it can become problematic as you enter the workplace and have access to credit because you can go into a debt spiral. In turn, you may experience financial stress and struggle to achieve your long-term financial goals.

Not Prioritizing Savings

If you fail to prioritize your savings, you may find yourself unprepared for emergencies or unable to achieve your goals. It's crucial to set aside a portion of your income for savings regularly.

Overlooking the Importance of a Budget

A budget helps you track your spending, prioritize expenses, and ensure you are living within your means. Without a budget, it's easy to overspend and lose sight of your goals.

Mindless Expenses

Mindless spending refers to spending without thinking about the long-term impact on your finances. It includes impulse purchases and unnecessary expenses. Frequently, you're bound to regret these expenses after they happen, but by then, it's too late to get your money back.

Late Bill Payments

If you pay a bill late, it may result in extra fees and interest charges which adds unnecessary costs to your expenses. These extra costs were not included in your original budget, so it makes the impact even bigger. It's important to pay your bills on time to avoid these additional expenses.

Minimum Payments

Creditors expect you to make frequent payments on your debt, usually weekly or monthly. You can choose to pay the minimum amount or pay more than that. If you only pay the minimum amount, your debt continues to increase through high-interest charges and that can prolong the time it takes to pay off the debt.

It's better to pay more than the minimum to reduce your debt faster.

Spending on Wants

Unnecessary items or services can waste your valuable financial resources. These expenses would be on items you don't need for your survival. To spend mindfully, your money should go to essential items rather than nice-to-have items.

Where to Spend Money

So, what should you spend your money on? I would suggest the following:

- **Education.** Money spent on education is an investment that can lead to long-term benefits like higher earning potential and career advancement. You can pursue a degree, attend workshops, or take online courses.
- **Travel.** Travel, within reason, can broaden your horizons, expose you to new cultures, and create lasting memories.
- **Investments.** Investing your money wisely can help you build wealth over time. Consider stocks, bonds, or mutual funds, depending on your financial goals and risk tolerance.
- **Experiences.** Money spent on experiences, such as concerts or sporting events, provides personal fulfillment, memories, and value beyond that of material possessions.
- **Health and fitness.** If you invest in your health and fitness, you can have a better quality of life and be healthier overall.

Where Not to Spend Money

Of course, there are also things you shouldn't be spending money on, as follows:

- **Alcohol.** Excessive spending on alcohol can strain your finances and affect your health and well-being negatively.
- **Designer clothes.** While it's fine to splurge on quality clothing occasionally, overspending on designer labels or trendy items can lead to unnecessary expenses.
- **Technology you don't need.** Constantly upgrading to the latest gadgets or devices can be costly, so evaluate your technology needs carefully.
- **A brand new vehicle.** A reliable car is essential (if you don't have other transport) but a brand new car is a significant expense. A used or certified pre-owned car is a better option to save money and insurance costs.

The Best Way to Track Expenses

It's important to track your expenses for effective financial management and to achieve your goals. Here are some methods and tools to help you track your expenses:

Expense Journals

Use an expense journal to record all your expenses manually. This method requires discipline but can provide a detailed insight into your spending habits. Write down the date, amount, and category for each expense. It will help you understand where your money is going and identify areas where you can cut back.

Check Your Statements

Regularly review your bank and credit card statements to track your spending. Most statements categorize expenses which makes it easy to identify where your money is going. Look for any discrepancies or unauthorized transactions that may indicate fraud or errors.

Receipts

Save all your receipts and review them periodically to verify your expenses and ensure they align with your budget. Identify any unnecessary or impulse purchases to avoid in the future. Receipts also serve as a backup in case you need to dispute a charge.

Expense-Tracking Apps

Many apps are available to help you track your expenses effortlessly. These apps categorize your expenses, provide spending insights, and often sync with your bank accounts and credit cards for automatic expense tracking. We looked at some of these apps in Chapter 3.

Other Expense Trackers

Besides apps, consider using online tools and software designed for expense tracking. Some banks have these features built into their mobile and online banking platforms. Ask your bank if that is the case or search online for a different tool.

Categorize Your Expenses

Understand your spending patterns better by categorizing your expenses. Common categories include housing, transportation, groceries, utilities, personal care, and entertainment. These categories are similar to the ones used in a budget. Review the categories to see where you are spending the most money and identify areas where you can cut back.

Activate SMS or App Alerts

Many banks offer SMS or app alerts for transactions. Activate this service to receive real-time notifications of your expenses to help you stay updated on your spending. This can help you track your expenses more efficiently.

Tools and Apps

Several other tools and apps can be useful for tracking expenses, such as the following:

- While simple, the Notes app can be used to track basic expenses. Create a note for each month and record your expenses manually.
- Create a custom expense tracking spreadsheet in Google Sheets. Include columns for date, amount, category, and notes for each expense.
- Spendee offers comprehensive expense-tracking features, including budgeting tools and expense categorization. It provides a clear overview and helps you make informed spending decisions.
- Mint is a free app that provides a holistic view of your financial health. It tracks expenses, creates budgets, and has built-in reminders.
- Goodbudget uses the envelope method to track expenses. It allows you to allocate funds to different categories and track your spending against your budget.

THE FEAR OF MISSING OUT

Have you ever spent money on something because your friends were doing it? It could be splurging on tickets for a show or buying the latest sneakers. Some people call this peer pressure, but you can also consider it FOMO, which stands for "fear of missing out." It's the feeling or perception that other people have more fun, live better lives, or experience a richer life than you do, so you believe you need to do it too. This fear often arises from seeing others' experiences on social media or hearing about their activities and achievements.

FOMO can have a significant impact on your finances. It can lead to impulsive and unnecessary spending as you try to keep up with others or seek experiences you believe will make you feel more included or fulfilled. It can also cause overspending on experiences such as dining out, attending events, or traveling, even when it may not align with goals or budget. The result: financial stress, debt, and an inability to achieve your long-term goals.

To prevent FOMO, identify your values and priorities to determine what experiences or purchases are truly important to you. Develop a budget that reflects your financial goals and allocate funds for experiences and purchases that are important to you while ensuring you stay within your means. Be grateful for what you have rather than focusing on what others have to reduce feelings of inadequacy that may lead to unnecessary spending. Limit your exposure to social media if it triggers feelings of FOMO. Remember, social media often portrays a curated version of reality and does not reflect the full picture of a person's life. Instead of focusing on material possessions, prioritize experiences that bring you genuine happiness and fulfillment. This can help you make more meaningful and satisfying choices with your money.

TAKE CONTROL OF YOUR SPENDING

It's time to take control of your money and stop spending money unnecessarily.

Reasons You Can't Stop Spending Money

Why are you spending money? It's possibly due to several reasons. Go through the possibilities below and identify the ones that resonate with you.

Paying With Plastic

Using debit cards or other forms of plastic payment (such as gift cards) can make it easier to overspend. The convenience of not handing over physical cash can lead to impulse buys. For example, you may see a sale in-store and buy items you don't really need because it's easy to swipe your card.

Lack of Self-Awareness

Not being fully aware of your spending habits can lead to overspending. If you're not mindful of where your money is going, you may not realize how much you're spending. For instance, you might buy a coffee daily without realizing how much it adds up monthly.

Shopping to Feel Better

If you turn to retail therapy as a way to cope with stress, anxiety, or other emotional issues, you may spend on unnecessary items for temporary happiness. You don't need these items, but your brain believes you do.

Not Tracking Your Spending

Financial mismanagement may happen because you do not track your spending. If you don't keep track of expenses, you don't know where your money is going, making it easier to overspend.

Six Questions to Ask Yourself Before Spending

Many people find it difficult to stop spending at the drop of a hat. You need to decide to pause and think about every purchase. Use the questions below to help you do that:

1. Do I need this, or do I just want it?

Differentiate between essential purchases and impulse buys by considering whether the item will add value to your life or if it's a fleeting desire. If the answer is "want," consider whether the purchase aligns with your goals and if you can afford it without compromising your budget.

2. Can I afford it without going into debt?

Your purchase should be within your financial means and not require debt. If you can't afford it without going into debt, it's wise to reconsider the purchase or find a more affordable alternative.

3. Will this purchase bring me long-term satisfaction?

Evaluate the long-term value of the purchase and whether it will still be valuable to you in the future. If the purchase is likely to bring you long-term satisfaction, it may be worth the investment. However, if it's a short-lived trend, you may be better off skipping it.

4. Have I researched cheaper alternatives?

Research alternatives to help you find a more cost-effective option without compromising on quality. A cheaper alternative that meets your needs can help you avoid overspending.

5. Is this purchase in line with my financial goals?

Align your purchase with your financial goals to ensure your money achieves what matters most to you. Any purchase that doesn't align with your goals is possibly an unnecessary expense.

6. Can I wait before making this purchase?

Consider whether you really need this item right now. If you can wait 24 hours, a week, or a month before buying it, then it might be a want. Take some time to think it over and ensure it's a wise decision.

Ways to Avoid Unnecessary Spending

Besides the questions above, there are other ways to help you stop spending money, as we'll look at below.

Delay Gratification

When you feel the urge to make a purchase, try delaying the decision for at least 24 hours. This gives you time to consider whether the purchase is necessary. You may find that the desire to buy fades over time, saving you money in the long run.

Challenge Yourself

Set specific, achievable goals to motivate yourself to save money and avoid unnecessary spending. For example, you could challenge yourself to save a certain amount of money each month or to pay off a credit card debt by a certain deadline.

Save Your Bonuses

If you receive a bonus or some unexpected money, put it directly into your savings account or use it to pay off debt. This can help you avoid the temptation to spend the extra money on nonessential items and instead use it to improve your financial situation.

Fun and Frugal Activities

Look for activities that are both enjoyable and affordable. You could explore local parks, have a picnic, or attend free community events. By finding fun activities that don't cost a lot of money, you can satisfy your desire for entertainment without overspending.

Get an Accountability Buddy

Find a friend, family member, or financial advisor who can hold you accountable for your spending. Share your financial goals with them and ask them to check in with you regularly to see how you're doing. They can also encourage you to stick to your budget.

Make Meals at Home

Cook your meals at home as much as possible because restaurants and takeout can be expensive. Plan your meals in advance, make a grocery list, and only buy those items when you go shopping.

Set a Shopping Limit

Before you go shopping, decide how much money you are willing to spend, and on what, and stick to that limit. It might be a good idea to use cash instead of a debit card, as this can help you avoid overspending. If you find yourself tempted to exceed your limit, remind yourself of your financial goals and the importance of sticking to your budget.

Cancel Subscriptions

Review your monthly subscriptions and cancel any that you no longer use or need. It could be magazine subscriptions, streaming services, or gym memberships. This frees up extra money in your budget for more worthy purchases or savings.

IMPULSE BUYING

I have to admit that I have a bad spending habit: I like to buy an iced coffee when I go grocery shopping. It's an impulse buy, something I buy without planning or considering the consequences of it beforehand. Impulse buys often involve spur-of-the-moment decisions based on immediate desires or emotions, rather than rational thoughts or needs. Do you have an impulse-buying tendency? What is it you like to get without a second thought? It could be candy, gum, energy drinks, clothing, video games, candles, home decor, toys, books, coffee and takeout, or other items to treat yourself. It doesn't help that retailers strategically place these items close to the checkout line or slap them with sale stickers. It's difficult to resist those purchases, but you need to if you want to protect your finances.

The Psychology Behind Impulse Buying

Impulse buys seem to happen by accident, but there are psychological reasons supporting it. Specifically, it comes down to emotional triggers, limited financial experience, and social influence.

Emotional triggers such as advertising, promotions, or product displays can evoke feelings like excitement, happiness, or desire. These emotions can override rational decision-making, and before you know it, you've added an unplanned item to your cart. For example, a limited-time offer can create a sense of urgency and prompt you to buy something immediately.

Limited financial experience can contribute to impulse buying. If you don't have much experience managing your finances, you may be more susceptible to impulsive spending. You may not fully understand the long-term consequences of your purchases or may not have strong budgeting skills. Luckily, as you're busy educating yourself by reading this book, you're on the right path to improving your daily finances.

Finally, social influence plays a role because you may be influenced by friends, celebrities, or social media influencers to buy things. Seeing others purchase certain products or engage in certain behaviors can create a sense of social pressure or FOMO to do the same.

The Negative Impact of Impulse Buying

Impulse purchases have negative consequences, simply because you are doing something that has financial consequences. Purchasing items on a whim without considering your budget can quickly add up, leaving you with less money for essential expenses or savings. But, there are other consequences too. After the initial thrill of an impulse purchase wears off, you may experience feelings of regret or guilt, especially if the purchase was unnecessary. This can hinder your savings goals, as money spent impulsively could have been saved for more important expenses or future plans.

Impulse buys can also contribute to clutter and disorganization in your home, specifically in small spaces, which can cause stress and anxiety. Additionally, impulse buying can become a habit that's difficult to break, and that may lead to ongoing financial problems.

It can also strain relationships, particularly if your spending habits affect the finances of someone else. Recognizing and addressing impulse buying behavior is important to avoid these negative consequences and maintain financial well-being.

How to Avoid Impulse Buys

You now know what the problem is with impulse purchases. With that in mind, let's move on to some strategies to minimize impulse buying:

- The most effective way to stop impulse buying is to avoid situations where you're likely to be tempted. This could mean unsubscribing from email newsletters, avoiding online shopping when you're bored, or steering clear of your favorite shopping spots.
- Use cash instead of cards because you become more aware of how much you are spending and on what.
- Avoid shopping when you're feeling emotional, stressed, or tired.
- If you feel the urge to make an impulse purchase, postpone it for 24 hours to see if the urge fades.
- Try a no-spend challenge where you commit to not spending money on nonessential items for a week or month.
- Find support from friends or family, and ask them to encourage you to save and hold you accountable for your purchases.

By implementing these strategies, you can reduce your impulsive tendencies and make more intentional purchasing decisions.

EXERCISE

Keep a spending journal for 30 days to help you gain insights into your spending patterns.

1. Get a notebook or create a spreadsheet where you can record your expenses.
2. Each day, write down your expenses (even the small ones). Add the date, amount, and what the expense was for.
3. Start categorizing your expenses after a few days.
4. Set aside time each week to review your spending journal. Look for patterns and trends. Are there categories where you consistently overspend? Are there areas where you can cut back?
5. Set financial goals based on the insights from your spending journal. Create a plan to reach these goals.
6. Based on your review, make adjustments to your spending habits.

The art of mindful spending isn't about deprivation but rather about making choices that align with your financial goals and values. It's about enjoying a fulfilling life while maintaining control over your finances. In the next chapter, we will explore the world of saving, a fundamental aspect of financial success.

THE SAVINGS ROAD MAP

> *"The habit of saving is itself an education. It fosters every virtue, teaches self-denial, cultivates the sense of order, trains forethought, and so broadens the mind."*
>
> — T. T. MUNGER

Do you have a bit of money stashed away somewhere? Some people call it a rainy day fund; others simply refer to it as savings. No matter what you call it, saving is a fundamental element of financial success. Saving was important to me early on because I wanted to save for retirement, create an emergency fund, and have some money for larger items. How about you?

THE POWER OF SAVINGS

Ask anyone about their financial goals, and I'm pretty sure saving money will be high on that list. But why is it important? Why should you start saving money? And how much is enough?

Why You Should Start Saving Now

Saving as a teenager or young adult provides security for your financial future. As you progress through life, your expenses are likely to increase. From higher education costs to starting a family and buying a home, each stage brings new financial responsibilities. By starting to save early, you'll be better prepared to handle these rising expenses without sacrificing your financial stability. If you save now, you can enjoy more financial freedom and security later in life, especially as you enter your 30s and beyond. You will have enough money to travel the world, buy property, or start a business. In short, saving gives you the flexibility to pursue your dreams and goals without financial stress.

As your income increases, it's easy to fall into the trap of increasing your spending along with it. This phenomenon, known as lifestyle inflation or creep, can make it difficult to save later on. However, you can establish a savings account now and live below your means to avoid this trap and build a solid foundation.

The earlier you start saving, the more time your money has to grow through the power of compound interest. Even small amounts saved now can grow into significant savings over time and help you achieve your financial goals faster, whether you are preparing for retirement or want to secure a down payment. Saving for retirement is important as it allows you to maintain your standard of living when you no longer have a rental income, but that's not possible if you don't start saving early on. Similarly, saving early can create a sizable down payment when you are ready to buy a home or invest in real estate.

Some savings options, such as retirement accounts offer tax benefits. By contributing to these accounts, you can reduce your taxable income, potentially saving you money on taxes. More importantly, you will develop valuable life skills to use your money wisely.

How Much to Save

The amount you should save depends on your financial goals, income, expenses, and timeline. However, a general guideline is to save at least 20% of your income. This can be divided into different savings goals, such as retirement, emergencies, and other financial objectives.

To determine how much you should save, use the following steps:

1. Define your short-term and long-term financial goals.
2. Calculate your monthly expenses, income, and how much money you have left over after financial obligations.
3. Create a budget that outlines how much you can realistically save each month.
4. Regularly review your savings goals and budget to ensure you are on track. Adjust your savings rate as necessary.

Barriers to Saving Money and How to Overcome Them

It's not always easy to save money, even if you have every intention to do so. Here are some reasons why this might be the case:

Too Much Debt

High levels of debt can make it challenging to save money as you need to make repayments and cover interest costs. It's best to focus on paying off high-interest debt first. Consider loan consolidation or seek professional advice to manage your debt more effectively. Once you've reduced your debt burden, you can redirect those payments toward savings.

Yourself

Sometimes, we can be our own worst enemies when it comes to saving money. A mindset shift is needed to overcome self-sabotage. Start by setting clear savings goals and creating a budget to track your progress. Automate your savings to help remove the temptation to spend impulsively.

High Housing Costs

Accommodation costs can consume a significant portion of your income, leaving less room for savings. To overcome this barrier, consider downsizing to a more affordable home or find ways to reduce your housing expenses, such as renting out a room.

Needless Spending

Impulse purchases and unnecessary expenses can derail your savings efforts. Track your spending and identify areas where you can cut back.

Poor Financial Literacy

Without a basic understanding of personal finance, it can be challenging to make informed decisions about saving and investing. But, thankfully, you are already taking steps to educate yourself by reading this book.

Tips to Make Saving Fun

It can be easier to save if you make it fun. Here are some ideas to do so:

- Get an accountability buddy by partnering with a friend or family member who also wants to save.

- Turn saving money into a game by setting up a savings challenge.
- Break your savings goals into smaller milestones and reward yourself each time you reach one.
- Instead of spending money on expensive activities, find new hobbies and simple pleasures to bring you joy.
- Look for ways to increase your income or save money on everyday expenses.
- Treat yourself occasionally when you reach a savings goal or milestone.

SET SAVINGS GOALS

I've already mentioned that financial goals are important, and savings goals are no different. A clear goal gives you a reason to save and keeps you motivated to stick to your plan, especially during challenging times. Goals help you prioritize your spending and identify areas where you can cut back to save more money. They also provide a way to measure progress and celebrate your achievements along the way, which can boost your confidence and motivation.

How to Set and Achieve Savings Goals

You can create savings goals and work toward them by using the following process:

1. Identify your short-term and long-term savings goals.
2. Rewrite your goals in the SMART format. You can check Chapter 1 for the specific steps.
3. Break your goals into milestones.
4. Create a savings plan that outlines how much you need to save each month.

5. Review your progress frequently and adjust your strategy as necessary.

Saving Strategies to Prioritize Different Financial Goals

It can be difficult to save money, but you can do it. Try some of these strategies to give your savings a boost:

Automate Your Savings

Set up automatic transfers from your normal bank account to your savings account. This way, you can prioritize your goals without thinking about them constantly. Automated savings can help build your savings more efficiently and make progress toward your goals faster.

Address High-Interest Debts First

If you have debts, prioritize paying them off first, then focus on other goals. High-interest debts can accumulate quickly and hinder your ability to save. Once paid off, redirect those payments to your savings account.

Save for Different Goals and Rank Them Too

It's important to save for different goals simultaneously, such as retirement, a vacation, or a down payment. Rank your savings goals in order of priority and allocate your resources in order of importance. This allows you to get closer to achieving your goals without sacrificing one for the other.

Use Multiple Savings Accounts

Consider using multiple savings accounts to help you reach your goals. This way, you can track your progress for each goal separately and avoid dipping into funds that were put aside for specific purposes.

Savings Accounts

In Chapter 4, I told you more about the different types of savings accounts. You need to decide which one will work best for your goals; you could even consider getting different types of accounts. For example, you may choose a certificate of deposit to help you save for a down payment over several years. In contrast, if you have a short-term savings goal, a money market or regular savings account might be the best option so that you have easy access to your money.

Why Put Money in Savings Accounts

The idea of saving makes sense, but maybe you still think there's no harm in just leaving your money in a checking account. Well, you need to understand that savings accounts have distinct advantages. For one, they offer interest rates on your money which allows it to grow over time. While interest rates may be relatively low, they are still higher than those of checking accounts. Usually, savings accounts are insured up to a certain limit by the Federal Deposit Insurance Corporation (FIDC) in the United States. This insurance protects your money in case the bank fails. If you keep your savings separate from your everyday checking account, you will be less tempted to spend it. This creates a barrier between your spending money and your savings, helping you to maintain financial discipline.

SET UP AN EMERGENCY FUND

Life is unpredictable, and unexpected expenses can arise at any time. Your car might break down and need urgent repairs, or maybe you lose your job but still need to pay your monthly accounts. An emergency fund allows you to cover these expenses without going into debt. You can consider it a financial buffer that cushions your fall. Knowing you have a financial security net can reduce stress and anxiety which allows you to focus on other aspects of your life.

How Much to Save

The general rule is that you should save three to six month's worth of living expenses in your emergency fund; however, the exact amount may vary based on your circumstances. For example, if your monthly expenses add up to $3,000, then your emergency fund should contain $9,000 to $18,000.

When to Use Your Emergency Fund

Your emergency fund is only for genuine emergencies, such as those mentioned earlier. Emergencies are only based on needs, such as affordable housing and food. It should not be used for wants like buying a luxury car or dining out. If an expense is not essential or can be planned for in advance, it should not be funded from your emergency fund. Your emergency fund will be depleted easily if you use it for nonemergencies, and that can leave you vulnerable in case of a true emergency. It's also important to replenish your emergency fund if you do use it so that you have protection for future unexpected expenses.

Rules for an Emergency Fund

An emergency fund needs to be handled carefully so that it can grow and be available when you need it. It helps to create rules or guidelines for yourself to ensure you stick to the plan. Let's go over some rules that worked for me. You can use these rules yourself or come up with your own.

Have a Specific Goal

A specific savings goal (like an amount or how many months you plan to save) provides a clear target to aim for. It can help you stay motivated and focused on building your fund to its target amount. Originally, I was still staying with my parents, so I only had a small savings goal, but I knew I wanted to save three months of rent before I moved out of the house.

Stick to the Benchmark

Don't try to complicate your saving efforts for your emergency fund. Stick to the benchmark of three to six months of living expenses, but realize that it will take longer than this to build up your fund because you will only be saving a small amount monthly. I focused on saving up three months' living expenses first —it took me about 15 months—and then kept saving half of what I originally did to build up the fund even more.

Keep It Liquid

Your emergency fund should be easily accessible when you need it. This means keeping it in a liquid form, which is a fancy way of saying it can "flow" to you easily. A normal savings account is a good option as you can withdraw money quickly when needed.

Opt for High-Interest Accounts

While the primary purpose of an emergency fund is to provide financial security, it's also important to maximize the growth of your savings. Keep your emergency fund in a high-interest savings account, even if it costs slightly more in fees.

Remember Your Why

It wasn't easy to save for my emergency fund; I wanted to use the money, not look at it. Whenever I got tempted to spend the money, I would remind myself why I was saving it in the first place. If necessary, write down your reasons for saving so that you have a constant reminder.

Steps to Set Up an Emergency Fund

To set up your emergency fund, you need to follow similar steps to what we have discussed previously in this book. Let's go through the process:

1. Calculate your monthly expenses by adding both your fixed monthly expenses and variable monthly expenses together.
2. Based on your monthly expenses, set a savings goal for your emergency fund. Remember it should be three to six months' worth of living expenses.
3. Open a separate savings account dedicated to your emergency fund.
4. Set up automatic transfers to your emergency fund so you can save effortlessly.
5. Review your budget and emergency fund balance frequently to determine if adjustments are necessary.

Here's a bonus tip: Look for ways to reduce your expenses and increase your income, then funnel all the extra money into your emergency fund. You can cut back on nonessential spending, sell items you no longer need, or start a side hustle. Take all the money you don't need for daily expenses and add it to your emergency fund. It might be a sacrifice right now, but it will be worth it when you really need that money.

SAVE FOR YOUR RETIREMENT

Have you thought about retirement? It may be a strange thing to think of when you've just started your first job, but it's so important to consider how you will live when you no longer work. So what does your retirement look like? For me, I knew I wanted to travel the world and socialize frequently with friends and family. When I thought about it some more, I realized that both of those things could be classified as wants. I wasn't thinking about where I would live, how I would earn an income, or how I would pay for my travels and social events. How much would I even need to retire comfortably? Can you understand why you need to think about your retirement now already?

By saving early for your retirement, your money has more time to grow through the power of compound interest. This means the interest you earn on your savings also earns interest, which accelerates your savings growth over time. You can invest in retirement accounts, such as 401(k)s or IRAs, and benefit from the long-term market growth. If you save early, you have more flexibility in how much you need to save each month to reach your retirement goals. You can take advantage of lower contribution amounts early on, which can be easier to manage with other financial obligations. Lower risk is associated with saving early because you can take a more conservative approach and have more time to recover from potential losses, which protects your retirement savings from market volatility. In the end, a substantial retirement savings fund can provide you with greater financial security later on in life. It ensures you have enough to cover your expenses and enjoy a comfortable retirement lifestyle.

Do the Math

Let's do the math to see how saving early on can lead to a better retirement savings amount compared to starting later. In the first scenario, we are going to look at a retirement account started at the age of 25, and in the second, an account started at age 35. In both cases, the monthly contribution is $200, the interest rate is 7% per annum (year), and the retirement age is 65. An online savings calculator was used to calculate the total savings.

	Scenario 1: Start at 25	Scenario 2: Start at 35
Monthly contribution	$200	$200
Annual interest rate	7%	7%
Retirement age	65	65
Number of years to save	40	30
Total contributions	$96,000	$72,000
Total savings at retirement	$669,615.82	$311,027.41

As you can see, the extra contributions over 10 years do increase the total contributions, but it has a much bigger impact on the total savings amount. The large growth seen in Scenario 1 comes from the extra time the savings have to enjoy compound growth. The longer your money has to grow, the more you can accumulate over time.

Simple Tips to Start

So, how do you start saving for retirement? Here are some ideas:

Contribute to Employer-Matched Retirement Plans

One of the simplest ways to save for retirement is to contribute to an employer-matched retirement plan if that is something you have access to. Keep in mind that you might only have this benefit once you are employed full-time. Many employers offer matching contributions up to a certain percentage of your salary. For example, if you contribute 3% of your salary to a retirement plan, then your employer might contribute 3% too, which doubles the amount you are saving monthly without any additional effort.

Consider Your Time Horizon and Risk Tolerance

Think about how long it will be until you retire and how comfortable you are with market fluctuations—this is your risk tolerance. Since you are young, you have more time to save and may feel comfortable investing in high-risk retirement accounts for a few years before applying a more conservative approach.

Increase Contributions Annually

As your income increases over time, consider increasing your retirement contributions too, or at least every year. Even small increases can have a significant impact on your long-term savings. Usually, retirement contributions are automated to ensure you save a little bit every month. For most retirement accounts, you can choose to have your contributions increased by a set percentage every year.

Get Creative

You may need to be creative to find some extra cash for retirement savings. You can opt for some traditional options like reducing your spending or finding a higher-paying job. Many retirement accounts also allow you to make lump-sum payments to the account occasionally, so you can use that opportunity to increase your savings. Consider asking for money for your birthday and adding that to your retirement account, or you could use any bonuses you get from work to boost your savings.

Strategies to Save for Retirement

The best retirement savings strategy for you depends on your individual circumstances, including your income, tax situation, and retirement goals. We are going to go over a few options now, but it's best to consult a financial advisor to determine the best approach for you.

IRAs

An IRA is a retirement savings account created for individuals and consists of either a Roth IRA or a traditional IRA. A Roth IRA is made with after-tax dollars, so you don't get a tax deduction for your contributions. However, qualified withdrawals (for contributions and earnings) in retirement are tax-free. Roth IRAs also offer flexible withdrawings before retirement age.

Contributions to a traditional IRA are made with pre-tax dollars, which allows you to deduct your contributions from your taxable income. When you make withdrawals, you will need to pay tax at your ordinary income tax rate. Traditional IRAs also have required minimum distributions (payouts to you) starting at age 72.

401(k) Plans

A 401(k) is an employer-sponsored retirement savings plan that allows you to contribute a portion of your salary to your retirement account. Usually, these contributions are made with pre-tax dollars which reduces your taxable income. Employers may also match a portion of your contributions to increase your retirement savings.

Traditional Pension Plans

A traditional pension plan is a retirement plan provided by an employer that guarantees a specified monthly benefit upon retirement. The benefit amount is typically based on a combination of factors, including years of service and salary history. Pension plans are funded by your employer and are not dependent on your contributions, making them different from 401(k) plans and IRAs.

TACKLE INFLATION ON SAVINGS

The other day, I went grocery shopping. I knew how much money I had to spend, but I couldn't believe how few items I could get for that amount. A few years ago, I could buy much more! You've probably experienced the same thing. What I am talking about is inflation. Inflation is the rate at which the general level of prices for goods and services rises, which leads to a decrease in purchasing power. In other words, as inflation rises, the price of items increases and the value of your money decreases, so it takes more money to buy the same goods and services.

The Impact of Inflation on Savings

Inflation erodes the purchasing power of your savings over time. This means that the amount you have saved now will have a lower value when you retire, and that's why it's so important to start saving early and in high-interest accounts. Your savings' growth rate should at least match the rate of inflation, otherwise, you effectively lose money.

For example, if inflation is 3% per year, and an item costs $100 today, it could cost $103 a year from now. Now, think of it in terms of savings. Technically, you need to save more than you think you do in order to beat inflation. One way to do this is to look for a high-interest savings account, such as one that offers 4% interest per year. Since this percentage is higher than the inflation rate, you are still growing your money.

How to Beat Inflation

Inflation will always be there, but there are ways to mitigate its impact on your savings.

- Invest in a diversified portfolio of stocks, as they tend to provide higher returns than inflation over the long term.
- Real estate can be a hedge against inflation, as property values and rental income tend to increase with inflation.
- Treasury inflation-protected securities (TIPS) are bonds issued by the U.S. Treasury and are indexed to inflation, which guarantees a return above the inflation rate.
- Diversify your investments across different asset classes, such as stocks, bonds, and real estate.

More importantly, remember to regularly review your savings and investment strategy as well as individual accounts to ensure they keep up with inflation. Adjust your strategy as needed to maximize your savings.

EXERCISE

Have you heard about savings games or challenges? They are ways to help you save more effectively by adding an element of fun. Choose one of the following games and use it to increase your savings:

Bank Your Change

Find a jar or piggy bank and commit to adding all your loose change and dollar bills to it. Whenever you go shopping and get change, add it to the jar immediately when you get home. You can save until the jar is full or for a set period of time, like a year. At the end of that time, take all your change to the bank and deposit it into your savings account.

Shop Against the Clock

Impulse shopping can ruin your savings, so this game is meant to take away the temptation. Write down your shopping list, then set a timer when you get to the store. You need to get all the items on your list and head to the checkout line at that time. This way, you don't have time to look for other items that aren't on your shopping list.

52 Cards

A normal deck of cards contains 52 cards; that's the same number of weeks in a year! Choose a value for each kind of card—for example, a King can be worth $15. At the end of each week, draw a random card from the deck, and add the assigned amount of dollars to your savings account.

Bank Your Savings

With this shopping game, you aren't searching for additional income to use for your savings; instead, you are turning to your current expenses to find the extra money. Look at your budget and compare it to how much you spent. If you have money left over, add it to your savings account. You can break this down into even smaller pieces. For example, if you budgeted $50 for a night out with friends but only used $46, move the rest of the money to your savings. It may seem like a small amount, but all those little bits add up quickly.

Use Your Age

If you are looking for a way to increase your savings every year, then the age game is perfect for you. Every month, save the same number of dollars as your age. If you are 16, save $16 per month. If you are 22, save $22 per month.

To succeed financially, you need to commit to saving and retirement planning for the future. Set goals, find ways to increase your savings, and stick to the plan. In the next chapter, we'll take this a step further and consider investments. We'll explore the various investment options available to you, understand the concept of risk and return, and learn how to make informed investment decisions.

INVESTING MADE SIMPLE

> *"The biggest risk of all is not taking one."*
>
> — MELLODY HOBSON

One step up from saving is investing. It's the process of putting your money into assets with the hope that it grows more than it would in a traditional savings account. You may not be able to invest (yet), but I want to tell you how strategic investment choices can enable you to build wealth. That can get you closer to your financial goals!

THE MAGIC OF COMPOUND INTEREST

Compound interest is like a magic trick for your money. It's the process where your investment earns money, and then that money earns even more money. Over time, this snowball effect can turn a small investment into a substantial sum.

Let's say you invest $1,000. If your investment grows by 8% in the first year, you'd have $1,080. But in the second year, that 8% growth is on the full $1,080—not just on the initial $1,000—so your investment will be worth $1,166.40. This process continues over and over again, which is the compounding effect. After 30 years, your initial investment will be worth more than $10,000! The longer your money compounds, the faster it grows.

To maximize the effects of compounding, invest early and consistently. The earlier you start, the more time your money has to grow. Even small, regular investments can grow into a significant sum over time. Another way to maximize the effect of compounding is to reinvest your earnings. Instead of cashing out your gains, reinvest them back into your portfolio.

But you may be wondering if investments are worth it all. I promise you they are, and the younger you start, the better. When you invest early, you have the option to retire early. By building a substantial investment portfolio over time, you may be able to achieve financial independence sooner than you think. You can also take advantage of lower-cost investment options, such as index funds or exchange-traded funds (ETFs). These investments typically have lower fees compared to actively managed funds, which can help maximize your returns over time.

As a young investor, you can take more risks within your investment portfolio because you have more time to recover from any potential losses. A high-risk investment has the possibility of earning higher returns more quickly, but if the investment doesn't do as well as planned, your funds can recover as you have many more years to grow your money.

INVESTMENT BASICS

The basic idea of investing is that you place money in some kind of asset with the hopes of achieving exponential growth over time. But there is more to think about. In this section, we are going to be talking about all the things to consider before you choose an investment.

Types of Investment Risks

Investment risks are like bumps and turns on a road—things that can affect how your investments perform. Just like how traffic, weather, or road conditions can impact your journey, investment risks can affect how your money grows or shrinks.

- Market risk is the risk that the value of your investments will go down because of changes in the market due to factors like economic conditions, political events, or changes in investor sentiment.
- Credit risk is the risk that the company or entity you've invested in won't be able to pay its debts if it goes bankrupt or faces financial difficulties.
- Concentration risk is the risk of having too much of your money invested in one type of asset, market, or company. If that asset or market performs poorly, it could have a big impact on your overall portfolio.
- Horizon risk is the risk that your investment foals or time horizon may not align with the performance of your investments, so you may not get the returns expected.
- Inflation risk is the risk that the value of your money will decrease over time due to rising prices. Your purchasing power can be eroded if your investments don't keep up with inflation.

- Reinvestment risk is the risk that you won't be able to reinvest your investment returns at the same rate of return as your original investment, which happens if interest rates or market conditions change.

If you understand these risks, you can look out for them and make more informed decisions about your investments. You can then take steps to manage these risks and protect your investment portfolio.

Profit From Inflation

In the previous chapter, we discussed inflation and how it decreases your purchasing power over time. Inflation can impact your investment because the returns may not keep up with inflation, leading to a decrease in real value. You have to be creative to overcome inflation risk.

One way to combat inflation risk is through diversification. By spreading your investments across different asset classes, such as stocks, bonds, real estate, and commodities, you can reduce the impact of inflation on your overall portfolio. Real estate is often considered a good option since property values and rental income tend to increase with inflation. TIPS—a type of government bond, as we briefly covered in the last chapter—will protect your principal investment which provides a guaranteed return.

Investment options in international markets can also help mitigate inflation risks. With global diversification, you can access markets that may be less affected by domestic inflation rates. If you are uncertain about domestic or international markets, consider investing in stocks and equities. Companies can raise prices in line with inflation which can help protect your portfolio against inflation risks.

How to Measure Investment Risks and Returns

Remember how I said that investment risks are similar to traveling on a bumpy road? Well, you can estimate investment risks and returns much like you would check the weather before your trip. It's not an exact science, but calculating risks and returns can give you a better picture of how your investments are doing and how risky they are.

It's important to calculate risks and returns because it helps you make better decisions about your investments. By understanding the risks involved, you can adjust your investment strategy to match your risk tolerance. It also allows you to track your progress toward your financial goals.

Calculate Returns

To calculate your investment return, subtract the initial investment amount from the current (or final) value of the investment, then divide it by the initial investment amount. Multiply the result by 100 to get a percentage return.

For example, if you invested $1,000 and it grew to $1,200, your return would be ($1,200-$1,000)/$1,000, which equals 0.2 or 20%.

Calculate Risk

It's a bit more challenging to measure investment risk because you never know what might happen in the future. One way to measure investment risk is to look at the volatility of your investment. Volatility measures how much the value of your investment goes up and down over time. Higher volatility means higher risk. To calculate volatility, you can use the standard deviation of your investment's return to give you an idea of how much the returns vary from the average return.

Another option is to look at the performance of an investment before you invest in it. Check the company's financial statement to see its stock value, profits, and other performance measures. Usually, they will report the values for two or three years at a time which gives you a comparison tool. Alternatively, talk to a financial advisor who can tell you more about the investment options you are looking at. They will be able to provide you with the history of the fund or stock and help you ascertain how risky they are.

Investment Tips

Before you run out to invest your money, go over these tips to help you make the most of your investment:

Audit Your Finances

It's crucial to assess your financial situation before you make any investment. Take note of your income, expenses, debts, and savings, then decide if you can invest and how much you are comfortable investing. For instance, if you are still building your emergency fund, you should focus on that first before you invest.

You Don't Have to Be an Expert

You don't need to be a financial expert or have a bunch of knowledge before you become an investor. Many resources, such as books, online courses, and financial advisors, can help you learn the basics of investing. Start with the basics and gradually build your knowledge over time.

Set Investment Goals

Define your investment goals based on your financial objectives, such as saving for retirement, buying a home, or funding your college education. Your goals will determine your investment strategy and risk tolerance. For example, you may need college funds soon, so it would be best to go for a low-risk investment as you don't have time to make up for potential losses.

Choose Your Investment Vehicles

An investment vehicle is simply the type of investment you decide on. It includes stocks, bonds, mutual funds, ETFs, and real estate. Each investment vehicle has its own risk-return profile, so choose investments that align with your goals and risk tolerance.

Understand Your Risk Tolerance

Any investment strategy needs to consider risk tolerance, which is how much risk you are willing to take with your money. Consider factors such as your age, financial goals, and comfort level with risk. A higher risk tolerance may lead to higher potential returns but also higher volatility. You can take this kind of risk while you are young, even if it is with just a small percentage of your money.

Determine the Amount You Want to Invest

Calculate how much money you can comfortably invest without jeopardizing your financial stability. Think about things like your budget, savings, and other financial obligations. Consider your situation right now and what it could be six months from now, or even a year. Will you need some more money then or can you afford to go without some of your luxuries?

What Kind of Investor Do You Want to Be?

There are different types of investors, including conservative, moderate, and aggressive. These link back to your risk tolerance and investment goals. A conservative investor will invest a bit of money in a low-risk vehicle. An aggressive investor is someone who doesn't mind losing a bit of money because they know they will make it up over the long term, so they invest in high-risk options. A moderate investor is somewhere in between. Where do you think you will fit in?

Build Your Portfolio

Once you clearly understand your financial situation, goals, and risk tolerance, you can build your investment portfolio. Choose one or two investment options to investigate more, and make a decision on what your first investment will be, even if it's still a long way off. Later on, diversify your portfolio across different asset classes to spread risk and optimize returns.

Choose the Right Investment Option

It's time to pick your investments! You might not be able to invest right now, but you will get an opportunity in the future. But thinking about your options can help you figure out which investment vehicles are for you.

Create a Financial Road Map

By now, you already know that every financial decision starts with setting goals. The same goes for investments. Identify your short-term and long-term financial goals that can be assisted with the growth of investments. It could be to buy a home, fund your education, or retire comfortably. Let your goals guide your investment decisions.

Determine Your Comfort Zone

Understand your risk tolerance and how it affects your choice of investments. Consider things like your age, financial goals, and how comfortable you are with market fluctuations. If you're risk-averse, you may prefer more conservative investments, while if you're comfortable with risk, you may opt for higher-risk, higher-return investments.

Consider Future Spending

Estimate your future spending needs and how much you'll need to save to meet those needs. Remember to include your wants in these calculations. Take into account inflation, lifestyle changes, and unexpected expenses. All of these things impact your cash flow and investment abilities.

Plan Your Investment Timeline

Your investment timeline, or how long you plan to invest, will impact your investment choices. If you're investing for the long term, you may be able to take on more risk for potentially higher returns. If you're investing for the short term, you may prefer more stable, low-risk investments. Factor that into your timeline.

Hands-On vs Hands-Off

Consider how involved you want to be in the management of your investments. Some people prefer a hands-on approach and actively manage their portfolios while also researching investment opportunities. Others may prefer a more passive approach, such as investing in index funds or getting their information from a financial advisor. Determine your level of involvement; you can always change this up as you go through life.

Examples

Many investment opportunities exist. We've already discussed CDs and high-yield savings which are ideal for short-term goals, but other options exist too.

- **Bonds** are debt securities issued by governments or corporations. They pay interest periodically and return the principal at maturity, making them a great option to generate income and preserve capital.
- **Funds** pool money from multiple investors to invest in a diversified portfolio of stocks, bonds, or other securities. They offer diversification and professional management which is a hands-off option.
- **Stocks** represent ownership in a company, as you buy a little bit of it. They offer the potential high returns but are high risk, so you must be in it for the long term.
- **Real estate** investments involve buying properties to generate retail income or profit from appreciation. They can provide steady income and long-term capital growth but require significant management.

Each investment option has its own risk-return profile. Consider your goals, risk tolerance, and investment timeline when choosing where to invest your money.

Diversify Your Portfolio

Diversification is the process of spreading your money across multiple investments.

Benefits of Diversification

Portfolio diversification reduces risk. By spreading your money across different asset classes, industries, and geographic regions, you can help reduce the impact of market volatility on your investments. When one investment underperforms, others may perform better, which balances your overall returns.

Diversification can potentially enhance your overall returns. Since you invest in many assets, you can capture gains from different market sectors and take advantage of growth opportunities. A diversified portfolio can provide more stable and consistent returns over time, compared to a concentrated portfolio that is heavily reliant on a few investments.

How Much to Diversify

The level of diversification depends on your risk tolerance, investment goals, and time horizon. Generally, you want to spread your investments across different asset classes and within each asset class to help reduce risk. This could mean that you invest in a different investment vehicle each time you have some money available.

Ways to Diversify

A diverse portfolio is like a colorful puzzle that consists of many parts to create a bigger picture. For me, it meant wise asset allocation, choosing several sectors, and considering different countries.

- **Asset allocation:** Allocate your investments across different asset classes, such as stocks, bonds, cash, and real estate, based on your risk tolerance.
- **Sector diversification:** Invest in different industry sectors (for example, technology, healthcare, and consumer goods) to reduce the impact of sector-specific risks.
- **Geographic diversification:** Spread your investments across several geographic regions to reduce country-specific risks and take advantage of global growth opportunities.

Diversification does not eliminate the risk of investment losses, but it can help mitigate risks and improve the overall performance of your portfolio. Regularly review and adjust your diversification strategy to ensure it remains aligned with your financial goals and risk tolerance.

Protect Your Money

Investing can be a great way to grow your wealth. However, I have to warn you that rookie mistakes can lead to losses. Sure, there are risks, but I'm talking about errors in judgment and strategy, so let's talk about what you need to avoid.

Lack of Research

Without thorough research, you might make poor decisions. Always research the company, market, and investment strategy before committing your money. The more you learn about a potential investment opportunity, the better your chances of success and risk reduction.

Emotional Investments

If you let emotions, such as fear or greed, dictate your investment decisions, it may lead to buying investments at high prices and selling them at lower values, resulting in losses. It's important to stay disciplined and stick to your investment plan. Similarly, don't make an emotional decision and invest in something because your friends or family are; you still need to do your own research instead of relying on an emotional connection.

Trying to Time the Market

When you time the market, you try to predict market movements and use them to decide how and when to move your money. It's a challenging approach because you need to stay aware of what's happening all the time, and there is no guarantee that you will be correct. Instead, focus on long-term investment goals and stay invested through the market's ups and downs.

Ignorance About Fees

Every investment costs something. There will be fees, especially if you are using an investment manager to take charge of your portfolio. Placing your money in the investment and withdrawing it will also incur costs. Be mindful of fees associated with your investments and consider low-cost alternatives.

Chasing Trends

People—especially through social media—talk about investments frequently, and this can give rise to some interesting trends. But that doesn't mean you should follow them. If you don't do your own research, you are putting yourself at risk. Stick to your investment plan, do your research, and avoid impulse decisions based on hype.

INVEST IN THE STOCK MARKET

The stock market is a place where buyers and sellers trade shares of publicly listed companies. It provides a platform for companies to raise capital by issuing shares while investors use this platform to buy and sell shares. Think about some of your favorite brands or companies. It could be Pepsi-Cola, Frito-Lay, or Nike. In all likelihood, the company you are thinking of is listed on the stock exchange. The stock market is also known as the equity market and plays a crucial role in the economy as it facilitates investment and capital formation.

How to Invest in the Stock Market

Here's the truth: You can invest in the stock market! You don't need some strange degree or accreditation; all you need is yourself and a strategy. I propose the following:

1. Learn the basics of investing, including how the stock market works, different investment strategies, and how to research stocks.
2. Define your investment goals.
3. Develop a plan that aligns with your goals, risk tolerance, and time horizon.
4. Begin with a small amount of money that you can afford to invest. Consider index funds or ETFs as a starting point.
5. Choose a reputable brokerage firm and open a brokerage account. Compare fees, customer service, and investment options before selecting a broker.
6. Conduct thorough research on individual stocks before investing by considering factors like the company's financial health, management team, industry trends, and valuation.
7. Buy your chosen stocks.
8. Monitor your investment portfolio and make adjustments as needed based on your goals and market conditions.

Tips for Stock Market Investment

Are you ready to invest? Let's recap the tips we discussed throughout this chapter to ensure you are off to a solid start:

- Learn as much as possible about investments to create a solid foundation of financial knowledge.
- Diversify your portfolio to reduce risk.

- Consider investing in dividend-paying stocks for passive income.
- Do not try to time the market.
- Focus on long-term growth.

The Cost of Investing in Stocks

Stock investing comes with costs such as brokerage fees, commissions, and taxes. It's important to factor these costs into your investment decisions and look for ways to minimize them. Talk to several brokerage firms to determine the costs of their services as well as the general stock market costs, and include these in your risk and return calculations.

The Best Stocks for Beginners

As a beginner, you need to find trustworthy stock options. It's often recommended to start with well-established companies with a track record of stable performance. Look for companies with strong balance sheets, consistent earnings growth, and a history of paying dividends.

Stock Market Investment Mistakes to Avoid

Stock market investment can be rewarding, but it's important to avoid common mistakes that can lead to losses. The key mistakes to look out for have already been covered in previous chapters.

- Investing without a clear plan or strategy can lead to aimless decisions. It's much better to have investment goals, consider risk tolerance, and have an investment timeline.

- Another mistake is not diversifying your portfolio, as that means you are putting all your eggs in one basket.
- A failure to research and analyze individual stocks is an error too. You need to conduct thorough research on company fundamentals, financial health, and industry trends before investing.
- Overtrading—the frequent buying and selling of stock—can lead to high transaction costs and reduced returns.

If you avoid these common mistakes and stay focused on your long-term financial goals, you can minimize risks and build a successful portfolio over time.

EXERCISE

You may have heard of virtual (online) trading platforms before. I've played around with them myself, and I can tell you that they are the ideal place for you to explore too. The Virtual Investment Challenge is an exciting opportunity to learn more about investing. It offers a risk-free environment where you can practice making investment decisions and learn valuable lessons along the way.

1. **Choose a virtual investment platform.** Do an online search for free investment simulation software and select one to use. These platforms are for educational purposes, and most reputable financial websites will have one.
2. **Set up a virtual portfolio.** Open a virtual investment portfolio with a starting amount of virtual money (for example, $100,000). Some platforms will have a starting amount set out already. The platform should allow you to invest in stocks, bonds, mutual funds, or other investment vehicles.

3. **Research and select investments.** Now that your portfolio is open, research different investment options, and select the ones that make sense to you. Choose between the different investment vehicles, and diversify your portfolio to spread risk.
4. **Monitor and adjust.** Monitor the performance of your portfolio over your chosen time period. It could be every few weeks or months. Track how your virtual performance is doing, including gains and losses.
5. **Learn from mistakes.** It's okay to make mistakes in this virtual challenge. Use any losses as an opportunity to learn and adjust your investment strategies.
6. **Compete or collaborate.** Most virtual challenge platforms allow you to compete with other participants to see who can grow their portfolio the most. Alternatively, it can be a collaborative effort, where you can discuss strategies with other participants and learn from each other.
7. **Reflect and share.** At the end of the challenge, reflect on your experiences. What did you learn about investments? Which strategies worked and which didn't? Share your insights with friends or family to improve your learning experience.

The Virtual Investment Challenge is a fun and engaging way to learn about investments. It's also a valuable opportunity to develop important financial skills that can benefit you in the future.

I hope you've learned more about investment opportunities, risk and return, and the insights necessary to make informed investment decisions. By understanding the potential for financial growth and wealth building through investments, you're better prepared for your financial journey ahead. Now, it's time to move to the final chapter, where we shift our focus to debt management.

Debt can be a double-edged sword, so you have to understand how to use it wisely.

DEBT-FREE JOURNEY

> *"Debt is the slavery of the free."*
>
> — PUBLILIUS SYRUS

Have you ever owed something to someone? I remember the first time I owed someone money. I was about 11, and my dad had been warning me not to kick the ball so close to the house because I was going to break a window. But did I listen? No. And, of course, the ball soon smashed through the window. My dad shook his head and told me he warned me that this would happen. I'm sure this has happened to most of us. But then my dad told me that I would have to pay to replace the window. I had no idea how I would do it, but he told me that he would pay for the replacement and I would owe him the money. I could earn money by washing the car and doing other odd jobs around the house. It wasn't fun at all. I couldn't do what I wanted to because I had to make up the money first.

The same feelings and experiences apply to debt. When you incur debt, you use someone else's money and have to pay it back somehow. You are limited because you can't spend money on other things until your debt is paid off. In this chapter, we are discussing debt, how to use it wisely, and how to repay existing debt.

THE IMPORTANCE OF CREDIT

Credit (also called debt) is important because it allows you to access loans and credit cards, which provide financial flexibility and the ability to make purchases or deal with emergencies when you don't have enough cash. A positive credit history—built over time—enables you to qualify for loans, rent apartments, and even secure employment. Additionally, a good credit score can lead to lower interest rates on loans and credits, saving you money over time. With good credit, you can negotiate more favorable credit terms and higher credit limits. Overall, credit plays a big role in your financial well-being, and provides access to financial resources and opportunities that can help you achieve your goals.

Credit Scores

A credit score is a numerical representation of your creditworthiness, which indicates how likely you are to repay money you borrow. Lenders, such as banks and credit card companies, use credit scores to assess the risk of lending to you. The score is based on information from your credit report, which includes your credit history and current credit situation.

Think about it this way: If you have a friend who asks to borrow $50 from you, but you know they still owe you $20 from three months ago, will you lend them the extra money? Probably not because the risk that you won't get your money back anytime soon is high. But what if your friend asks to borrow $20 occasionally and always repays the money within two weeks? That is a low-risk friend as you know the likelihood of getting your money back is high. Creditors think about you in the same way, and your credit score represents your risk profile.

Credit Score Grading

A credit score is a three-digit number ranging from 300 to 850, with higher scores indicating lower credit risk. In other words, the closer your credit score is to 850, the better your chances are of getting credit because lenders believe you will repay your debts, so you are a low-risk borrower. The most commonly used credit score is the FICO score, developed by the Fair Isaac Corporation. Other credit scoring models exist, but FICO scores are widely used by lenders.

Credit scores are typically graded as follows:

- 300–579: Poor
- 580–669: Fair
- 670–739: Good
- 740–799: Very good
- 800–850: Excellent

These grades may vary slightly depending on the scoring model used but it does give you a general idea.

How Credit Scores Work

Credit scores are calculated based on several factors, including your payment history, amounts owed, length of credit history, new credit, and types of credit used. The most significant factors affecting your score are your payment history and how much you owe. Think back to the example with your friend—you base your lending decisions on these factors too.

How to Build Your Credit Score From Scratch

Since you are still young, you probably don't have a credit score yet. You are starting from the ground up, which can seem like a challenge, but it's a good thing because the only way is up!

Here are some ways to build your credit score:

Become an Authorized User

Ask a family member or close friend with good credit to add you as an authorized user on their credit card. This can help you build credit as the other person's positive payment history is reported on your credit report. However, this is a huge responsibility, because you need to use the card responsibly and pay back what you owe, otherwise you can negatively impact both your credit history and the other person's. Additionally, if the other person doesn't make payments, it can affect you negatively, so decide carefully who you want to ask about this option.

Secured Credit Card

A secured credit card requires a security deposit which serves as your credit limit. For example, you can pay a security deposit of $200, and your limit is then $200. Use this card responsibly and make timely payments to help establish a positive credit history. If you don't make the payment, you lose your security deposit, but that will also reflect on your credit report.

Credit for Monthly Bill Payments

Some service providers report your monthly payments for utilities, rent, and cell phone bills to credit bureaus. Even gym contracts could be reported to credit bureaus, and all of these help to show you can make regular, on-time payments.

Credit Builder Loan

A credit builder loan is specifically designed for building credit history. You borrow a small amount, which is placed in a savings account. As you make payments, the lender reports your positive payment history to the credit bureaus. Once you've paid the full amount, you can access the funds in the savings account.

Monitor Your Credit Utilization

You need to keep your credit card balances low relative to your credit limit if you want it to have a positive effect on your credit score. Aim to use no more than 30% of your available credit.

Small Purchases Paid Off Quickly

A good way to build your credit score is to make low-value purchases using your credit card and then pay off the balance in full each month. For example, you can put $50 in your savings account for debt repayment specifically. You can then buy items to the value of $50 throughout the month, and use the $50 you set aside to pay the credit card bill. This shows you can use credit responsibly.

Use a Cosigner

If you're unable to qualify for a credit card or loan on your own, a cosigner with good credit can help you access credit. A cosigner accepts responsibility for your actions and commits to paying the account if you don't pay it. That's a big responsibility! You need to take responsibility for that credit card, otherwise you mess up the other person's credit report.

Check Your Credit Report

The only way to know if your credit score is improving is to check it regularly. You can check your report through one of the three major credit bureaus—Equifax, Experian, and TransUnion—to ensure it's accurate. There are also credit tracking apps that you can use to monitor any changes in your credit score. These apps usually send you a monthly report that identifies your credit score, any changes, new credit checks by lenders, and any outstanding debts.

GOOD VS BAD DEBT

Bad debt refers to borrowing money to purchase items that don't increase in value or generate long-term income. This type of debt typically carries high interest rates and can be detrimental to your financial health if you don't manage it carefully. For example, this could include using your credit card to pay for daily expenses like groceries or a night out. Another example of bad debt is a payday loan, which is a short-term, high-interest loan; you get the cash immediately, but it can be difficult to pay off the debt due to the high fees.

Good debt is used to finance investments that have the potential to increase in value or generate income over time. It is often considered an investment in your financial future. For instance, student loans are used to fund education which may result in a higher earning potential as your career advances. Similarly, a mortgage to purchase a home can be considered good debt as real estate tends to increase in value over time.

DEBT AND DEBT MANAGEMENT

Now that you understand debt better, it's time to talk a bit more about the different options available to you and how to use debt properly.

Loan Types for Young Adults

You may be wondering whether a loan is worth it at all, or you might already know that you have no choice but to get credit to achieve your goals. Some of the reasons you can get a loan are to finance your education, purchase a car for transport to school and work, cover emergency expenses or unexpected financial setbacks, or establish and build a credit history.

Here are some loans you might consider:

- student loans to help cover the cost of higher education, including tuition, books, and living expenses
- personal loans to use for various purposes such as home improvements or car purchases
- auto loans to purchase a vehicle, with the vehicle serving as collateral for the loan
- credit builder loans to help you build or improve your credit history
- payday loans for emergency expenses

Before you take out a loan, you need to think about it very carefully. Go through all the documentation the lender gives you to understand the terms of the loan, including interest rates, fees, and repayment terms. Determine if you can really afford the monthly payments. If your budget is tight right now, it may not be that easy to accommodate the repayments. Consider alternative options and the impact of borrowing on your financial future. Alternative options include scholarships and grants for education expenses, financial aid programs, or building your savings to cover expenses.

Remember, it can be challenging to get a loan since you are still so young. That's mostly due to a limited credit history and limited income. If you do not have established credit, it's harder to qualify for loans. Lenders may also be hesitant to lend to you if you don't have a decent income or if your employment situation is unstable. You can increase your chances of getting loans by using existing credit responsibly and making timely payments. Additionally, you can increase your income or apply again after having a stable job for several months.

Avoid Unnecessary Loans

A loan should be your last resort. It's always best to save for big expenses, but I know that life happens and that loans may be unavoidable. However, loans should be for things that improve the outlook of your financial future. You need to avoid unnecessary loans for living expenses. Here is how to do just that:

- Avoid eating out and cook your meals at home to save money.
- Buy secondhand textbooks or rent them to avoid borrowing money for educational expenses.
- Keep track of your expenses to identify areas where you can cut back.
- Avoid the temptation to overspend or keep up with extravagant lifestyles; instead, live within your means and stick to your budget.
- Don't fall for "buy now, pay later" schemes, as they are

convenient in the short term but they can lead to long-term debt if not managed carefully.

Finally, if you have built an emergency fund over time, you should be able to cover unexpected or emergency expenses. This is why you have an emergency fund in the first place, so always work on saving for it first.

CREDIT CARDS 101

Credit cards are financial tools that allow you to borrow money from a financial institution to make purchases, with the agreement to repay the borrowed amount (plus interest), usually on a monthly basis. When you use a credit card, you are essentially borrowing money from the card issuer, up to a predetermined limit. For instance, your card limit could be $100, $2,000, or more. You can use the card to make purchases in stores, online, or over the phone. At the end of each billing cycle, you receive a statement with details about your transactions and the amount you owe. You have the option to pay off the full balance, make a minimum payment, or a combination of both. If you do owe anything on your credit card, interest will be charged on the balance.

The Pros and Cons of Credit Cards

In all likelihood, you will get a credit card at some point in your life. Before you do, you may want to know the benefits and disadvantages of getting one.

The pros of credit cards include convenience since they are widely accepted and can be used for various purchases. Responsible credit card use can help you establish and improve your credit score. Many credit cards also offer rewards such as cashback, points, or miles that can be used for purchases. Some credit card issuers also offer other benefits like discounts at certain stores, so always check your documents carefully for how you can save.

The biggest con of credit cards is that they have high interest rates which can increase your balance rapidly and make repayments difficult. Credit cards also come with annual fees, late payment penalties, and other charges that can become expensive. The ease of using a credit card can also lead to overspending and accumulating debt. As a result, credit card mismanagement can decrease your credit score.

Types of Credit Cards

I decided to get a credit card with a small limit at the age of 21 to help build my credit history. Imagine my surprise when I was asked what type of credit card I wanted! I always thought there was just one kind of credit card. Apparently, there are several options, as follows:

- Rewards credit cards offer rewards, including points and cashback for using our card.
- Credit-building cards help anyone with a limited or poor credit history to establish or improve their score.
- Low-interest and balance transfer cards offer lower interest rates, which makes them suitable to reduce costs or consolidate debt.
- Travel rewards credit cards offer rewards such as points or miles that can be redeemed for travel-related expenses, such as flights or hotel stays.
- Student credit cards are designed for college students, have lower credit limits, and offer rewards tailored to student needs.

- Store credit cards are issued by specific retailers and offer benefits such as discounts or rewards for purchases made at the store.
- Secured credit cards require a security deposit, which serves as collateral and determines the credit limit. They are often used to build or rebuild credit.

Regardless of the type of credit card you get, you will pay credit card charges and fees. These may include an annual fee which is charged yearly for using the card. Interest is charged on any balance you carry from month to month. Late payment fees and over-limit fees may also apply if you exceed your credit card limit or fail to make timely payments. It's important to read the terms and conditions of the credit card agreement to understand all charges and fees associated with the card.

Get Your First Credit Card

Before you apply for a credit card, you need to understand exactly how they work and how they can impact your finances. Familiarize yourself with key terms such as the annual percentage rate (APR), credit limit, and fees. Assess your financial situation and determine if you're ready for the responsibility of managing a credit card.

To apply for a credit card, do the following:

1. Research different credit card options to identify one that suits our needs.
2. Visit the issuer's website or apply in person at a bank branch.
3. Fill out the application form with accurate information, including your income and personal details.

4. Wait for a decision. You may receive an instant decision or have to wait a few days for the issuer to review your application.
5. If your application is approved, review all the terms.
6. Sign for your credit card.

Use Your Credit Card Wisely

A credit card is a big responsibility, but it can be essential for building a positive credit history and avoiding debt. Next, I'd like to share a few tips with you to make the best of your credit card facility.

Start by making small, manageable purchases that you can pay off easily each month. Aim to pay off your full balance by the due date each month to avoid interest charges, as this will reflect positively on your credit report. If you're unable to pay off your full balance, try to pay more than the minimum payment to reduce your balance faster and minimize interest charges. It's also a good idea to set up alerts for your credit card to notify you of important events, such as approaching your credit limit to payment due dates.

Be cautious of where you use your credit card, regardless of whether it is online or in-store. Choose trusted merchants (stores) to avoid fraud and unauthorized charges. Aim to use a maximum of 30% of your available credit to avoid damaging your credit score. A low utilization ratio shows lenders you can manage credit responsibly. Finally, don't open multiple credit cards in a short period of time, as that can negatively impact your credit score.

STUDENT LOANS

A student loan is a loan you take out to fund your education. While often necessary, a student loan can have long-lasting effects on your life after college.

The Consequences of Student Loans

Student loans can create a significant financial burden and require you to allocate a portion of your income to monthly loan payments, limiting your ability to save for other financial goals. The financial strain of student loans can also delay your pursuit of other dreams, such as traveling or starting a business. You may also feel limited in your career choices and opt for higher-paying jobs rather than following your passion.

If you fail to repay your student loan, it will hurt your credit score which makes it harder to qualify for other types of credit in the future. It also makes it challenging to rent an apartment or secure certain jobs, such as those in the financial industry. The pressure of managing student loan debt can lead to stress and anxiety, impacting your mental health and overall well-being.

Alternatives to Student Loans

Instead of a student loan, there are other ways to pay for your education. These are as follows:

- Scholarships are merit-based or need-based financial awards offered by schools, private organizations, and government agencies that do not require repayment.
- Grants are need-based financial aid provided by the

federal or state government or colleges and don't require repayment.
- The Federal Work-Study program provides part-time jobs for undergraduate and graduate students with financial needs, allowing them to earn money to help pay for education expenses.
- Some colleges and universities offer tuition waivers to certain students, such as veterans and dependents of employees, which exempts them from paying part or all of their tuition fees.
- Some employers offer tuition reimbursement programs as part of their employee benefits.
- Stipends are fixed sums of money paid to students to help cover living expenses while they pursue their education. They are provided by colleges, research programs, or employers.
- Some employers offer sponsorship programs to help employees further their education, and these usually cover tuition expenses, provide paid time off for classes, or offer other forms of support.
- Many colleges and universities offer payment plans that allow students to spread out their tuition payments over time, making college more affordable and reducing the need for loans.

Strategies to Pay Off Your Student Loan

A student loan is a good thing because it is an investment in education for your future. But that means you need to complete your studies and pay back the loan.

Make Additional Payments

If you come into extra money, such as a tax refund or bonus, consider making a lump-sum payment toward your student loan. You can also make additional payments toward the principal amount of your loan to help pay it off faster. Even small payments can add up over time and reduce the total interest paid.

Ask for Help

Find out if your employer offers student loan repayment assistance as part of their benefits package. This is an option even if you joined the company after you finished your studies.

Take Advantage of Tax Deductions

You may be eligible for a tax deduction on your student loan, but that depends on your income and the amount of interest you've paid on your student loan. Although it doesn't affect how much you will pay right now, a tax deduction does help your overall financial situation.

Apply for Loan Forgiveness

If you work in a public service or certain other professions, you may be eligible for loan forgiveness programs. These programs forgive a portion of your student loans in exchange for a certain number of years of service.

STRATEGIES TO PAY OFF DEBT

Whether you have credit card debt, loans, or some other kind of credit, you want to pay it off as soon as possible. Right now, that may not seem like a problem, but you may find yourself with excessive debt in the future. These strategies can help you pay it off faster:

Snowball Method

With the snowball method, you pay off your debts from smallest to largest, regardless of interest rate. Make minimum payments on all debts except the smallest, on which you focus all extra funds. Once the smallest debt is paid off, you move to the next smallest, which creates a snowball effect. This method can provide a psychological boost as you see debts being eliminated quickly, motivating you to continue.

Debt Avalanche

The debt avalanche method prioritizes debts based on the interest rate, with the highest interest rate debt being paid off first. Make the monthly minimum payments on all your other accounts, and push any extra money into the debt with the highest interest rate. Once it is paid off, move to the one with the next highest interest rate. Over time, you pay off your debts and save on interest.

Debt Consolidation

Debt consolidation involves combining multiple debts into a single loan with a lower interest rate. This can simplify your debt repayment by having one monthly payment. Potentially, it can reduce the amount of interest you'll pay over time. However, be sure to carefully consider the terms and fees associated with debt consolidation to ensure it's the right option for you.

EXERCISE

Are you ready to take control of your finances and pay off your debts? You can do it with a debt paydown challenge to start your journey toward financial freedom. Just follow these steps:

1. Identify your current debts. Take stock of your current debts, including student loans, credit card debt, and personal loans. Note the outstanding balances and interest rates for each debt.
2. Set a debt payoff goal. Decide on a specific debt paydown goal, like paying off a certain percentage of a particular debt or becoming debt-free in a set timeframe.
3. Create a debt payoff plan. Allocate a portion of your income each month to paying down your debts and commit to adding any extra income to debt repayment.
4. Track your progress. Regularly track your progress by updating your balances and calculating how much debt you've paid off. This will help you stay motivated and focused on your goal.
5. Celebrate your milestones. No matter how small, celebrate your achievements. It could be paying off a certain debt or reaching a specific percentage of your debt paydown goal. Take time to acknowledge your progress and reward yourself.

Keeping the Game Alive

Now that you've learned all about how to achieve financial independence and save money, it's your turn to pass on this awesome knowledge and show other young folks where they can get the same help.

By sharing your honest thoughts about this book on Amazon, you'll help other teens and young adults find the guide they need. You'll show them how cool and important it is to be smart with money, just like you are now.

Thank you so much for your help! The journey of teaching personal finance to teens and young adults stays alive because of people like you who share what they've learned. You're really making a big difference!

Scan the QR code below to leave your review on Amazon

You're not just keeping the game alive; you're making it better for everyone. Thanks again!

CONCLUSION

We've reached the end of our journey into the world of financial literacy. Can you believe we are here already? Throughout this book, we've explored essential concepts that can shape your financial future. From the importance of starting early to understanding the value of saving, and making wise spending decisions to the role of debt, we've uncovered the difference wise money management can make in your life.

Financial literacy is about knowing what to do and taking action. The strategies and insights you've gained throughout these pages are the foundation upon which you can build a secure life. So, don't wait! Start applying these principles in your life today. Remember, mistakes are bound to happen. Don't break your mind about them; instead, embrace the failures, learn from them, and use them to propel yourself forward.

I want to leave you with a success story. Ellen, a colleague of mine, focused on her finances as soon as she graduated from high school. She opened a savings account and set aside a portion of her earnings from her part-time job. When she turned 18, Ellen applied for a student credit card and used it responsibly, paying off the balance in full each month to build her credit score. Ellen was careful about her spending and questioned herself if a purchase was a need or a want. She researched affordable college options and applied for scholarships and grants to avoid the need for student loans. By the time she graduated, Ellen had a solid credit history, minimal debt, and a financial plan for the future. Today, Ellen is financially secure, with a well-paying job and a comfortable savings cushion. She's grateful for the financial habits she developed early on. Ellen's story is a testament to the power of financial literacy, and you too can achieve financial success. It's never too early to start, so why not begin your financial journey today?

I hope this book has been enlightening and empowering. If you found it helpful, please consider leaving a review. Your feedback will help others discover the benefits of financial literacy and inspire me to continue creating content that makes a difference.

Thank you for letting me guide you on this journey! I wish you lots of financial success!

REFERENCES

Adams, K. (2022, April 24). *15 unconventional ways for students to make money.* Investopedia. https://www.investopedia.com/financial-edge/0909/14-unconventional-ways-for-students-to-make-money.aspx

Adams, R. (2024, January 14). *40+ ways to make money as a teenager [Fast + smart].* WealthUp. https://wealthup.com/ways-to-make-money-as-a-teenager/

Adams, R. (2024, January 10). *13 best banking apps for kids & teens.* WealthUp. https://wealthup.com/banking-apps-for-kids-and-teens/

The advantages of diversification. (n.d.). Schwab Moneywise. https://www.schwabmoneywise.com/essentials/the-advantages-of-diversification

Agatha. (2020, September 24). *8 biggest money traps to avoid in your 20s.* The Wealth Tribe. https://thewealthtribe.com/8-biggest-money-traps-to-avoid-in-your-20s/

Akinbinu, O. (2022, August 29). *Money mindset: What it is & why it is important.* LinkedIn. https://www.linkedin.com/pulse/money-mindset-what-why-important-funmi-akinbinu/

Artzberger, W. (2023, December 24). *Eight common investing mistakes to avoid.* Investopedia. https://www.investopedia.com/articles/stocks/07/beat_the_mistakes.asp

Ayoola, E. (2024, February 20). *The best budget apps for 2024.* Nerdwallet. https://www.nerdwallet.com/article/finance/best-budget-apps

Bakke, D. (2023, September 15). *The top 25 investing quotes of all time.* Investopedia. https://www.investopedia.com/financial-edge/0511/the-top-17-investing-quotes-of-all-time.aspx

Bank accounts for young adults—what do you really need? (2021, July 7). Elevations Credit Union. https://blog.elevationscu.com/bank-accounts-for-young-adults-what-do-you-really-need-prodch/

The benefits of investing early. (2023, February 27). Groww. https://groww.in/blog/early-investing

The benefits of tracking your spending habits. (2023, November 22). Hubble. https://www.myhubble.money/blog/the-benefits-of-tracking-your-spending-habits

Bennett, R. (2023, August 10). *Seven simple ways to build good money habits.* Bankrate. https://www.bankrate.com/banking/savings/ways-to-build-good-money-habits/

Bennett, R. (2023, June 7). *How to choose a bank: 8 steps to take.* Bankrate. https://www.bankrate.com/banking/how-to-choose-a-bank/

Bennett, R. (2023, April 13). Five saving strategies for financial goals. Bankrate. https://www.bankrate.com/banking/savings/savings-strategies-for-different-goals/

Birken, E. G. & Foreman, D. (2020, March 5). *How to budget in 7 simple steps.* Forbes. https://www.forbes.com/advisor/banking/how-to-budget-simple-steps/

Bozhinova, J. (2024, January 15). *Stop wasting money: quotes that will inspire you to save.* https://pawns.app/blog/stop-wasting-money-quotes-that-will-inspire-you-to-save/

Brennan, D. (2023, April 10). Benefits of a teenager getting a job. WebMD. https://www.webmd.com/parenting/benefits-of-a-teenager-getting-a-job

Brin, C. (2022, December 12). *Creative and fun ways to save money—saving money doesn't need to be boring!* HyperJar. https://hyperjar.com/blog/money-management-creative-and-fun-ways-to-save-money

Brown, K. (2023, May 11). *Try a money saving game! 15 grown-up savings games to try.* Clever Girl Finance. https://www.clevergirlfinance.com/saving-game/

Burnette, M. (2023, April 4). *Types of savings accounts: where to stow your cash.* Nerdwallet. https://www.nerdwallet.com/article/banking/types-of-savings-accounts

Callahan, C. (2022, September 20). *How student loans impact your life.* Credello. https://www.credello.com/student-loans/impacts-of-student-debt/

Caldwell, M. (2022, June 22). *Finance goals for your 20s.* The Balance. https://www.thebalancemoney.com/savings-goals-to-reach-in-your-20s-4113000

Cariaga, V., McFadden, A., & McNutt, E. (2023, November 30). *9 best high-yield savings accounts February 2024.* CNN. https://edition.cnn.com/cnn-underscored/money/high-yield-savings-accounts

Chafin, J. A. (2023, September 22). *5 simple budgeting methods to help you live your best life.* Lendingtree. https://www.lendingtree.com/student/simple-budget/

Chan, C. (n.d.). *What does it mean to set SMART financial goals?* Credit Counselling Society. https://nomoredebts.org/blog/budgeting-saving/what-does-it-mean-to-set-smart-financial-goals

Choosing the right investment option for you. (n.d.). CareSuper. https://www.caresuper.com.au/financial-education-hub/investments/investment-basics/choosing-the-right-investment-option-for-you

Chorpenning, A. (2024, January 12). *What is the snowball method?* Creditkarma. https://www.creditkarma.com/advice/i/what-is-the-snowball-method

Cruze, R. (2023, October 12). *How to stop spending money.* Ramsey. https://www.ramseysolutions.com/budgeting/the-cure-for-excessive-spending

REFERENCES | 151

Cruze, R. (2023, May 24). *How to change your money mindset.* Ramsey. https://www.ramseysolutions.com/budgeting/understanding-your-money-mindset

Cussen, M. P. (2022, September 13). *The top five ways to hedge against inflation.* Investopedia. https://www.investopedia.com/articles/investing/060916/top-5-ways-hedge-against-inflation.asp

Daly, L. (2022, December 25). *5 smart financial goals for 20-year-olds.* The Ascent. https://www.fool.com/the-ascent/personal-finance/articles/5-smart-financial-goals-for-20-year-olds/

DeNicola, L. (2023, June 14). *How to build credit from scratch.* Creditkarma. https://www.creditkarma.com/credit/i/how-to-build-credit-from-scratch

Davis, C. & Taube, S. (2024, February 8). *How to invest in stocks.* Nerdwallet. https://www.nerdwallet.com/article/investing/how-to-invest-in-stocks

Devaraj, S. (2023, October 9). *5 financial mistakes to avoid in your 20s and how investing can help.* Income. https://www.income.com.sg/blog/financial-mistakes-to-avoid-how-investing-can-help

Dore, K. (2023, September 11). *Best budgeting apps.* Investopedia. https://www.investopedia.com/best-budgeting-apps-5085405

Doyle, A. (2022, December 11). *Job search tips and advice for teens.* The Balance. https://www.thebalancemoney.com/tips-for-finding-a-job-for-teens-2058651

Educational expenses: needs vs wants. (2014, April 21). American Public University. https://apuedge.com/educational-expenses-needs-vs-wants/

Effects of inflation on investments. (2023, August 7). US Bank. https://www.usbank.com/financialiq/invest-your-money/investment-strategies/effects-of-inflation-on-investments

Eight important benefits of working while you're a student. (2022, August 17). Indeed. https://www.indeed.com/career-advice/career-development/working-student-benefits

11 money moves to master in your 20s. (n.d.). Truist. https://www.truist.com/money-mindset/principles/mind-money-connection/finance-goals-for-your-20s

11 types of credit cards. (2023, December 19). CapitalOne. https://www.capitalone.com/learn-grow/money-management/types-of-credit-cards/

Epstein, L. (2023, October 11). *10 tips for managing your student loan debt.* Investopedia. https://www.investopedia.com/articles/personal-finance/082115/10-tips-managing-your-student-loan-debt.asp

Etzel, N. (2022, June 30). *57% of young adults dread budgeting. Here's how to take the stress out of it.* The Ascent. https://www.fool.com/the-ascent/personal-finance/articles/57-of-young-adults-dread-budgeting-heres-how-to-take-the-stress-out-of-it/

Fay, B. (2022, April 18). *How to avoid landing in debt.* Debt. https://www.debt.org/advice/avoiding-debt/

Fay, B. (n.d.). *Good debt vs. bad debt.* Debt. https://www.debt.org/advice/good-vs-bad/

Fernando, J. (2023, December 24). *Financial literacy: what it is, and why it is so important.* Investopedia. https://www.investopedia.com/terms/f/financial-literacy.asp

Ferreira, N. M. (2020, February 16). *To all the entrepreneurs in their twenties.* Oberlo. https://www.oberlo.com/blog/entrepreneurs-in-their-twenties

Finance quotes. (n.d.). Good Reads. https://www.goodreads.com/quotes/tag/finance

Financial navigating in the current economy: Ten things to consider before you make investing decisions. (n.d.). US Securities and Exchange Commission. https://www.sec.gov/investor/pubs/tenthingstoconsider.htm

15 questions to ask before you buy anything. (n.d.). Living That Debt Free Life. https://www.livingthatdebtfreelife.com/home/15-questions-to-ask-before-you-buy-anything

50+ best money mindset quotes for attracting financial success. (n.d.). The Strive. https://thestrive.co/money-mindset-quotes/

Financial habits and norms. (n.d.). CFPB. https://www.consumerfinance.gov/consumer-tools/educator-tools/youth-financial-education/learn/financial-habits-norms/

Financial literacy. (n.d.). Wall Street Mojo. https://www.wallstreetmojo.com/financial-literacy/

Financial literacy: adding up the benefits of starting young. (2019, August 22). Georgia's Own. https://www.georgiasown.org/financial-literacy-adding-benefits-starting-young/

Financial literacy: 5 basic concepts to know. (2023, July 27). Capital One. https://www.capitalone.com/learn-grow/money-management/financial-literacy/

Five great reasons to save when you're young. (2021, January 6). National Bank. https://www.nbc.ca/personal/advice/savings-investment/benefits-of-saving-young.html

Five money habits to create this year. (n.d.). Fulton Bank. https://www.fultonbank.com/Education-Center/Trending/5-Money-Habits-to-Create

Five obstacles that can stand in your way when you're trying to save money. (2022, February 3). Due. https://due.com/obstacles-save-money/

Frankel, M. (2024, February 13). *How to invest in stock: A beginner's guide for getting started.* The Motley Fool. https://www.fool.com/investing/how-to-invest/stocks/

Fontinelle, A. (2024, January 8). *Debit card definition, fees, and how they work.* Investopedia. https://www.investopedia.com/terms/d/debitcard.asp

Fontinelle, A. (2024, January 1). *How to set financial goals for your future.* Investopedia. https://www.investopedia.com/articles/personal-finance/100516/setting-financial-goals/

Four things to know before opening a bank account. (n.d.). CBC Bank. https://www.cbcbank.com/opening-bank-account-guide

Gopalakrishnan, J. (n.d.). *Stock investment risk: understanding systematic and idiosyncratic risks.* Britannica Money. https://www.britannica.com/money/types-of-investment-risks

Gravier, E. (2024, January 2). *10 common money habits this CFP says his wealthy self-made millionaire clients have that normal people could copy.* CNBC. https://www.cnbc.com/select/money-habits-of-self-made-millionaires/

Green, H. (2022, October 3). *Tips for teenagers on finding that first job.* The Parents Website. https://theparentswebsite.com.au/tips-for-teenagers-on-finding-that-first-job/

Gross pay vs. net pay: What's the difference? (n.d.). ADP. https://www.adp.com/resources/articles-and-insights/articles/g/gross-pay-vs-net-pay

Grossman, A. L. (2023, February 16). *7 free teen budget worksheets & tools (Start your teenager budgeting).* Money Prodigy. https://www.moneyprodigy.com/teen-budget-worksheets/

Haan, K. (2023, Septembet 25). *Best expense tracker apps.* Investopedia. https://www.investopedia.com/best-expense-tracker-apps-5114591

Hagen, K. & Tretheway, C. (2024, February 8). *How to choose a bank.* The Ascent. https://www.fool.com/the-ascent/banks/how-to-choose-bank/

Hargrove, D. (2023, November 30). *70 business ideas for young adults: Avoid the get-rich-quick schemes and turn a profit.* Niche Pursuits. https://www.nichepursuits.com/business-ideas-for-young-adults/

Hausman, A. (2021, September 14). Building a startup in your 20s: benefits to starting early. Market Maven. https://www.hausmanmarketingletter.com/building-a-startup-in-your-20s-benefits-to-starting-early/

Here's why budgeting in your 20s is important and how to get started today! (2023, May 18). Finex Credit Union. https://www.finexcu.org/blog/heres-why-budgeting-in-your-20s-is-important-and-how-to-get-started-today

Honeycutt, B. (2023, April 11). *Savings goals: How to set and achieve them.* Forbes. https://www.forbes.com/advisor/banking/savings/savings-goals/

Horton, M. (2024, January 27). *What are some ways to minimize tax liability?* Investopedia. https://www.investopedia.com/ask/answers/040715/what-are-some-ways-minimize-tax-liability

How setting savings goals is important in financial management—tips to set savings goals from DNBC. (2023, January 11). DNBC. https://www.dnbcgroup.com/blog/how-setting-savings-goals-is-important-in-financial-management-tips-to-set-savings-goals-from-dnbc/

How to build an emergency fund. (2022, June 29). Investopedia. https://www.investopedia.com/personal-finance/how-to-build-emergency-fund/

How to file your federal income tax return. (n.d.). USA.gov. https://www.usa.gov/file-taxes

How to improve your credit score. (n.d.). Experian. https://www.experian.com/blogs/ask-experian/credit-education/improving-credit/improve-credit-score/

How to keep a spending journal. (2016, March 17). Quicken. https://www.quicken.com/blog/how-keep-spending-journal/

How to prevent 'FOMO' from wreaking havoc in your finances. (2016, June 13). CTV News. https://www.ctvnews.ca/5-things/how-to-prevent-fomo-from-wreaking-havoc-on-your-finances-1.2940958

How to prioritize savings and investing goals. (n.d.). Securian. https://www.securian.com/insights-tools/articles/how-to-prioritize-savings-and-investing-goals

How to shift your money mindset in five easy steps. (n.d.). Money Mentors. https://moneymentors.ca/money-tips/how-to-shift-your-money-mindset/

How to stop spending money. (n.d.). Money Mentors. https://moneymentors.ca/money-tips/8-tips-to-avoid-spending-money-on-wants/

How you should and shouldn't spend money in your 20s. (n.d.). Money Lover. https://note.moneylover.me/how-you-should-and-shouldnt-spend-money-in-your-20s/

The importance of saving at a young age. (n.d.). 3RC. https://3rc.co.za/the-importance-of-saving-at-a-young-age/

Impulse buying: How to avoid regrettable financial decisions in your 20s. (2023, August 10). HDFC Life. https://www.hdfclife.com/insurance-knowledge-centre/investment-for-future-planning/how-to-avoid-impulsive-buying-in-your-20s

IRS free file: Do your taxes for free. (n.d.). IRS. https://www.irs.gov/filing/free-file-do-your-federal-taxes-for-free

Jain, S. (2022, December 24). *5 financial mistakes I wish I avoided in my 20s.* The Economic Times. https://economictimes.indiatimes.com/markets/stocks/news/5-financial-mistakes-i-wish-i-avoided-in-my-20s/articleshow/96472742.cms?from=mdr

Jayakumar, A. (2023, November 2). *What is debt consolidation, and should I consolidate?* Nerdwallet. https://www.nerdwallet.com/article/finance/consolidate-debt

Johnson, H. D. (2022, September 27). *How to use your first credit card.* Bankrate. https://www.bankrate.com/finance/credit-cards/how-to-use-first-credit-card/

Jones, M. (2023, July 28). *10 tips to choose the best checking account.* Experian. https://www.experian.com/blogs/ask-experian/tips-to-choose-best-checking-account/

Juma, N. (2023, April 27). *110 money quotes celebrating financial literacy and independence.* Everyday Power. https://everydaypower.com/money-quotes/

Kaitlin. (n.d.). *The importance of setting financial goals.* The Simply Organized Home. https://www.thesimplyorganizedhome.com/one-income-wednesday-the-importance-of-setting-financial-goals/

Kirkham, E. (2023, February 23). *30 essential money habits*. Go BankingRates. https://www.gobankingrates.com/saving-money/budgeting/essential-money-habits/

Knisley, M. (2024, January 29). *7 reasons you should budget: Why is budgeting so important?* InCharge. https://www.incharge.org/financial-literacy/budgeting-saving/budgeting-benefits/

Kolesnikova, T. (2023, February 15). *10 tips for balancing work and school*. Studybay. https://studybay.com/blog/how-to-balance-work-and-studies/

Lake, R. (2023, December 20). *How do credit cards work?* Investopedia. https://www.investopedia.com/how-do-credit-cards-work-5025119

Lake, R. (2022, May 23). *How to make money as a teen*. The Balance. https://www.thebalancemoney.com/how-to-make-money-as-a-teen

Lake, R. & Foreman, D. (2021, May 13). *Are budgeting apps worth it?* Forbes. https://www.forbes.com/advisor/banking/are-budgeting-apps-worth-it/

Lake, R. & Stevens, T. (2023, June 12). *What do you need to open a bank account?* Forbes. https://www.forbes.com/advisor/banking/how-to-open-a-bank-account/

Lambarena, M. (2020, January 17). *How to choose a bank account: seek low fees, high rates*. Nerdwallet. https://www.nerdwallet.com/article/banking/how-to-choose-a-bank-account

Lamberg, E. (2023, May 21). *Why it's important to start a retirement plan in your 20s*. Fox Business. https://www.foxbusiness.com/personal-finance/why-important-start-retirement-plan-20s

LaPonsie, M. (2024, February 16). *22 legal secrets to help reduce your taxes*. US News. https://money.usnews.com/money/personal-finance/articles/legal-secrets-to-reducing-your-taxes

Lazar, A. (2023, November 27). *How to set SMART financial goals (with examples)*. Finmasters. https://finmasters.com/smart-financial-goals/#gref

Lee, D. (2022, December 13). *What is a budget strategy? 12 effective methods and tips*. Indeed. https://www.indeed.com/career-advice/career-development/budget-strategy

Leeds, P. (2022, November 3). *10 common stock investing mistakes to avoid*. The Balance. https://www.thebalancemoney.com/common-investing-mistakes-you-must-avoid-4104189

Luthi, B. (2023, May 16). *The complete guide to understanding credit scores*. Experian. https://www.experian.com/blogs/ask-experian/credit-education/score-basics/understanding-credit-scores/

Luthi, B. (2021, August 22). *7 ways to stick to your budget*. Experian. https://www.experian.com/blogs/ask-experian/ways-to-stay-on-budget/

Maharishi, M. (2022, April 21). *Understanding your first paycheck (and why it's so much smaller than you thought)*. CNBC. https://www.cnbc.com/2022/04/20/understanding-your-first-paycheck-and-why-its-so-much-smaller-than-you-thought

Matthews, K. L. (2024, January 16). *A beginner's guide to investing in the stock market*. Fortune. https://fortune.com/recommends/investing/how-to-start-investing/

McDonald, T. (2023, September 6). *9 money myths to stop believing today*. https://brookstonewealth.com/9-money-myths-stop-believing-today/

McGurran, B. (2021, June 8). *What is financial literacy and why is it important?* Experian. https://www.experian.com/blogs/ask-experian/what-is-financial-literacy-and-why-is-it-important/

Michael, A. (2023, November 15). *What inflation means for your investments*. Forbes. https://www.forbes.com/uk/advisor/investing/what-inflation-means-for-your-investments/

Mistakes to avoid in budgeting. (n.d.). 20s Finances. https://www.20sfinances.com/mistakesinbudgeting/

Money mindset: how important your attitude to money is. (2022, February 5). OVB. https://www.ovb.eu/english/blog/article/money-mindset-how-important-your-attitude-to-money-is.html

Money mindset: *How your attitude towards money impacts your financial success*. (2023, August 18). ICICI Direct. https://www.icicidirect.com/research/equity/finace/money-mindset-how-your-attitude-towards-money-impacts-your-financial-success

Murray, C. (2023, November 16). *How to start budgeting*. Money Under 30. https://www.moneyunder30.com/budgeting-in-your-20s/

Neidel, C. (2022, April 26). *Needs vs. wants: How to budget for both*. Nerdwallet. https://www.nerdwallet.com/article/finance/financial-needs-versus-wants

Nine good money habits for the new year. (2023, December 27). Discover. https://www.discover.com/personal-loans/resources/consolidate-debt/good-financial-habits/

Nine questions to ask before opening a bank account. (n.d.). Fulton Bank. https://www.fultonbank.com/Education-Center/Saving-and-Budgeting/Bank-account-questions

Nine tips to protect yourself while at the ATM. (n.d.). Jefferson Bank. https://www.jefferson-bank.com/learning-center/9-tips-to-protect-yourself-while-at-the-atm/

Noori, E. (2023, May 7). *Seven financial literacy basics we all need to know*. Clever Girl Finance. https://www.clevergirlfinance.com/financial-literacy-basics/

O'Shea. (2023, November 15). *Identity theft: What it is, how to prevent it, warning signs and tips*. Nerdwallet. https://www.nerdwallet.com/article/finance/how-to-prevent-identity-theft

O'Shea, B. & Schwahn, L. (2024, February 16). *Budgeting 101: How to budget money.* Nerdwallet. https://www.nerdwallet.com/article/finance/how-to-budget

Parks, J. (2017, April 19). *11 steps to starting a successful business in your 20s.* https://www.entrepreneur.com/starting-a-business/11-steps-to-starting-a-successful-business-in-your-20s/292854

Parys, S. & Orem, T. (2024, February 12). *How to file taxes: 2024 tax filing guide.* Nerdwallet. https://www.nerdwallet.com/article/taxes/tax-filing

Polglase, A. (2023, March 8). *How to set up a budget and stick to it.* HyperJar. https://hyperjar.com/blog/how-to-stick-to-a-budget

Porter, T. J. (2021, September 14). *5 reasons to use a budgeting app to manage your finances.* Money Crashers. https://www.moneycrashers.com/reasons-use-budgeting-app-manage-finances/

Powell, E. (2023, December 7). *Opening a bank account.* Go Compare. https://www.gocompare.com/current-accounts/opening-your-first-bank-account/

Pradhan, D. (2024, February 14). *What is mobile banking and how does it work?* Forbes. https://www.forbes.com/advisor/in/banking/what-is-mobile-banking/

Pritchard, J. (2022, November 22). *How to open a bank account and what you need to do it.* The Balance. https://www.thebalancemoney.com/how-can-i-easily-open-bank-accounts-315723

Pritchard, J. (2022, May 26). *How to check your bank balance online.* The Balance. https://www.thebalancemoney.com/check-your-bank-balance-online-315469

Reiner, M. (2022, January 14). *8 simple ways to trim unnecessary spending.* The Balance. https://www.thebalancemoney.com/how-to-trim-unnecessary-spending-4129673

Risk and return. (n.d.). CFI. https://corporatefinanceinstitute.com/resources/career-map/sell-side/capital-markets/risk-and-return/

Rose, S. (2023, October 24). *The 12 biggest financial mistakes to avoid in your 20s.* https://www.opploans.com/oppu/financial-literacy/financial-mistakes-to-avoid-in-your-20s/

Rounds, H. (2023, December 6). *Best student loan alternatives.* The College Investor. https://thecollegeinvestor.com/42315/best-student-loan-alternatives/

Sceithe, E. (2020, May 5). *Online and mobile banking tips for beginners.* Consumer Financial Protection Bureau. https://www.consumerfinance.gov/about-us/blog/online-mobile-banking-tips-beginners/

Seppi, M. (2024, January 12). *How to balance work and study?* International University of Applied Sciences. https://www.iu.org/en-za/blog/how-to/studying-and-working-at-the-same-time/

Seven barriers that keep us from saving money (and how to knock them down). (n.d.). Citizens. https://www.citizensbank.com/learning/barriers-to-saving-money.aspx

Seven money myths to stop believing today. (n.d.). Hudson Valley Credit Union. https://www.hvcu.org/learning-center/7-money-myths-to-stop-believing-today/

Seven reasons you need to set financial goals. (n.d.). Money Nuggets. https://www.moneynuggets.co.uk/important-to-set-financial-goals/

Seven simple ways to stop impulse buying: An actionable guide. (n.d.). Transfy. https://transfy.io/blog/7-simple-ways-to-stop-impulse-buying

Seven tips to manage your checking account. (2023, May 25). Discover. https://www.discover.com/online-banking/banking-topics/7-tips-to-manage-your-checking-account/

70 quotes on debt that will make you think. (2023, December 2). Gracious Quotes. https://graciousquotes.com/debt/

Sharkey, S. (2023, May 30). *SMART financial goals.* SmartAsset. https://smartasset.com/financial-advisor/smart-financial-goal-examples

Sillers, J. (n.d.). *Nine bad spending habits to break away from in your 20s.* Credit. https://credit.org/blog/9-bad-spending-habits-to-break-away-from-in-your-20s/

Six financial literacy principles. (n.d.). RBC Wealth Management. https://www.rbcwealthmanagement.com/en-ca/insights/6-financial-literacy-principles

Six reasons you should track your expenses as a student. (n.d.). Money Mini Blog. https://moneyminiblog.com/college/students-track-expenses/

Six simple steps to jump-start your emergency fund. (n.d.). Bank of America. https://bettermoneyhabits.bankofamerica.com/en/saving-budgeting/emergency-fund-tips

Six steps to creating a positive money mindset. (n.d.). Happy Bank. https://www.happybank.com/resources/six-steps-to-creating-a-positive-money-mindset

Silver, C. (2024, January 28). *The ultimate guide to financial literacy.* Investopedia. https://www.investopedia.com/guide-to-financial-literacy-4800530

Singh, A. V. (2023, July 12). *What financial literacy looks like today.* LinkedIn. https://www.linkedin.com/pulse/what-financial-literacy-looks-like-today-arjun-vir-singh/

Sky, E. M. (2023, April 3). *Financial literacy: 5 basic topics you need to know.* Quicken. https://www.quicken.com/blog/financial-literacy-basics/

Sokunbi, B. (2024, February 8). *11 key ways to improve your money mindset.* Clever Girl Finance. https://www.clevergirlfinance.com/how-you-can-improve-your-money-mindset/

Stevens, T. (2023, April 3). *How to get a debit card.* Forbes. https://www.forbes.com/advisor/banking/get-debit-card/

Strategies to pay down debt. (2023, September 25). Ontario Securities Commission. https://www.getsmarteraboutmoney.ca/learning-path/managing-debt/strategies-to-pay-down-debt/

Suresh, M. (2022, March 17). *How to track your finances.* Moneyview. https://moneyview.in/blog/how-to-track-your-finances/

Swenson, S. (2023, November 21). *What is money mindset?* The Motley Fool. https://www.fool.com/terms/m/money-mindset/

Sylvestre-Williams, R. (2022, January 6). *What is FOMO and how can you stop it from messing up your finances?* Sun Life. https://www.sunlife.ca/en/tools-and-resources/money-and-finances/managing-your-money/how-to-keep-the-fear-of-missing-out-from-messing-up-your-finances/

Tardi, C. (2023, December 11). *Debt avalanche: meaning, pros and cons, example.* Investopedia. https://www.investopedia.com/terms/d/debt-avalanche.asp

Tarpley, L. G. (2024, January 31). *Best banks in America—Banks with the best benefits.* Business Insider. https://www.businessinsider.com/personal-finance/best-banks

Teen guide: How to handle your first debit card. (n.d.). Bank of America. https://bettermoneyhabits.bankofamerica.com/en/saving-budgeting/managing-your-first-debit-card

10 strategies to avoid getting into debt. (n.d.). Central Bank. https://www.centralbank.net/learning-center/strategies-to-avoid-debt/

Tenny, J. (2022, April 4). *Survey finds 93% of teens believe financial knowledge and skills are needed to achieve their life goals.* BusinessWire. https://www.businesswire.com/news/home/20220404005339/en/Survey-Finds-93-of-Teens-Believe-Financial-Knowledge-and-Skills-Are-Needed-to-Achieve-Their-Life-Goals

Teoh, P. (2022, January 5). *10 financial goals to achieve in your 20s.* LinkedIn. https://www.linkedin.com/pulse/10-financial-goals-achieve-your-20s-pauline-teoh/

Tewari, A. (n.d.). *100 money affirmations for financial abundance and wealth.* Gratefulness. https://blog.gratefulness.me/money-affirmations/

Thangavelu, P. (2023, February 7). How inflation impacts your savings. Investopedia. https://www.investopedia.com/articles/investing/090715/how-inflation-affects-your-cash-savings

Three biggest challenges when making a monthly budget and how to overcome them. (2022, May 17). Jago. https://www.jago.com/en/blog/challenges-making-monthly-budget

Tomasetti, B. (2024, February 21). *Budgeting needs vs wants.* Carbon Collective. https://www.carboncollective.co/sustainable-investing/budgeting-needs-vs-wants

Tsosie, C. (2022, May 9). *11 things to know before getting your first credit card.* Nerdwallet. https://www.nerdwallet.com/article/credit-cards/things-to-know-first-credit-card

12 ways to earn extra money as a college student. (2023, January 31). Indeed. https://www.indeed.com/career-advice/finding-a-job/side-hustles-for-college-students

20 money affirmations for a positive mindset. (2022, March 8). The Currency. https://www.empower.com/the-currency/life/20-money-affirmations

Ubbenga, J. (2022, May 21). *Six questions to ask yourself before making a purchase.* Rich In What Matters. https://richinwhatmatters.com/2022/05/21/six-questions-to-ask-yourself-before-making-a-purchase/

Ward, J. (2023, June 9). *How to protect your savings from inflation when you're planning for retirement.* T.RowePrice. https://www.troweprice.com/personal-investing/resources/insights/how-help-protect-your-savings-from-inflation-when-youre-planning-for-retirement.html

Waugh, E. (2023, April 6). *Six ways to fight inflation and save money now.* Experian. https://www.experian.com/blogs/ask-experian/how-to-save-money-now-to-fight-inflation/

Waugh, E. (2022, April 11). *How to set SMART financial goals.* Experian. https://www.experian.com/blogs/ask-experian/how-to-set-smart-financial-goals/

Weliver, D. (2024, February 8). *Simple budget worksheet.* Money Under 30. https://www.moneyunder30.com/really-simple-budget-worksheet/

When do you get your first paycheck? A complete guide. (2023, June 9). Indeed. https://www.indeed.com/career-advice/pay-salary/when-do-you-get-your-first-paycheck

White, J. (2023, February 22). *100 motivational quotes about budgeting 2023.* Clarity. https://www.consultclarity.org/post/quotes-about-budgeting?expand_article=1

Why financial literacy is important? [10+ best usage]. (2023, January 21). Zoe Talent Solutions. https://zoetalentsolutions.com/why-financial-literacy-is-important/

Williams, T. (2023, December 29). *10 ways student debt can derail your life.* Investopedia. https://www.investopedia.com/articles/personal-finance/100515/10-ways-student-debt-can-destroy-your-life

Wilk, A. (2023, November 30). *Top 45 business ideas for 20-year olds [Updated for 2024].* Starter Story. https://www.starterstory.com/business-ideas-for-20-year-olds

Williams, T. (n.d.). *Financial literacy definition, benefits & importance.* Study.com. https://study.com/academy/lesson/financial-literacy-definition-benefits-importance.html#lesson

Wingo, L. (n.d.). *What business should I start? 6 factors to help you decide.* US Chamber. https://www.uschamber.com/co/start/startup/deciding-what-business-to-start

Working while in college: weighing the pros and cons. (2018, May 21). The College of St. Scholastica. https://www.css.edu/about/blog/working-while-in-college-weighing-the-pros-cons/

Yochim, D. & Ayoola, E. (2023, November 6). *How to save for retirement.* Nerdwallet. https://www.nerdwallet.com/article/investing/how-to-save-for-retirement

Yoshida, H. (2023, May 9). *Benefits of a properly diversified portfolio.* Forbes. https://www.forbes.com/sites/forbesfinancecouncil/2023/05/09/benefits-of-a-properly-diversified-portfolio/?sh=64dabd5f4e0c

Printed in Great Britain
by Amazon